A History of
Monasticism from
East to West

A History
of
Monasticism

FROM
EAST TO WEST

Mayeul de Dreuille OSB

Gracewing.

A Herder & Herder Book
The Crossroad Publishing Company
New York

First published in 1999
jointly by

Gracewing
2 Southern Ave
Leominster
Herefordshire
HR6 0QF

The Crossroad Publishing Company
370 Lexington Avenue
New York
NY 10017
USA

UK ISBN 0 85244 464 8

US ISBN 0 8245 1810 1
Library of Congress Catalog Number 99-72140

cum permissu Superiorum

Typesetting by
Action Publishing Technology Ltd, Gloucester, GL1 1SP

Printed in England by
Redwood Books,
Trowbridge, Wiltshire BA14 8RN

Contents

Introduction   vii

PART ONE

BORN BEFORE CHRIST: MONASTIC LIFE IN THE EAST

Ch.1 Hindu Monasticism   3
Ch.2 Buddhist Monasticism   28
Ch.3 Monasticism and Egyptian Religions   51
Ch.4 The Jewish Monastic Ideal: Qumran and the
      Therapeutes   58
Ch.5 Contacts between the East and Christian
      Monasticism   70

PART TWO

CHRISTIAN MONASTICISM

Ch.6 History   75
  1   Origins   75
  2   The Great Founders of the 4th Century   76
  3   The First Developments of Monastic
     Spirituality   84
  4   Monachism at the time of the Islamic
     expansion   89
  5   Western monasticism: the Benedictine
     centuries   93
  6   Western monasticism: decay and reform up
     to the French Revolution   96
  7   Eastern Monasticism   97
  8   Modern Renewal   99
  9   The History of Nuns   100

Ch.7 Themes of Monastic Spirituality   109
        1   Search for God   109
        2   Peace   111
        3   Silence   112
        4   Hospitality   114
        5   Work   116
        6   Various forms of monastic life   118
        7   Koinonia   120

Ch.8 Convergences   124

APPENDIX

I   Present State of the Monastic Orders in the
       Catholic Church   129

II   Chronology   130

Introduction

Some years ago, when I was in India, I published three books for the Benedictine monasteries of that country: one, *Monks Yesterday and Today*, giving the main themes of the monastic spirituality, a summary of the history of Christian monasticism and information about the Benedictine monasteries of India; the second, *From East to West, Men in Search of the Absolute*, a description of the monastic forms of life before Christ and a note on the Fathers of Christian monasticism; the third, on *Saint Benedict*. These are now out of print and, as they were appreciated in the West, and even in Africa, a new version was decided upon.

It was thought best to publish two new books rather than to reprint the old ones. The present volume gives the history of Asian monasticism with as much as possible of its spirituality and the historical framework of the Founders of Christian monasticism, whose spirituality is the object of the second volume.

I was led to include the study of non-Christian monasticism because it offers us a wealth of experience and information. People who engage in the search for the Absolute are faced with the same obstacles and try to surmount them in similar ways. It is not surprising, therefore, to see that problems, which seem to us typically modern and Christian (or even Roman Catholic) such as obedience, celibacy, the leadership of communities, rules about speech and silence, withdrawal from and openness to the outside world existed thousands of years ago in Egyptian, Hebrew, Hindu and Buddhist contexts. The difficulties experienced and the solutions adopted allow us to view our situation from a different angle and, perhaps, to recognise principles or sociological laws that throw light on it. Furthermore, all these religions are not simply phenomena of the past. Hinduism and Buddhism are actually living and active in Asia, and everyone knows that they are now acquiring an increasing importance in the West. The Christian religious in thus confronted everywhere with his likeness in other religions, and comparisons are inevitable.

To make these comparisons profitable, it seems to me that we must distinguish several degrees of thought or experience. The first is that of observances. Many similar practices concerning the way of life, asceticism and methods of meditation are found in the monastic life of all religions. These are based, it seems, on fundamental endowments of the human being, and their purpose is to make people attentive to the Reality beyond themselves. In this field, every religion, Christianity included, can profit from the experience of others and give them new life, as it interprets them in its own context.

A second level is that of the immediate motivation behind these practices. Here, we must note a great divergence of views and often, complete incompatibility. General as is the experience, the explanations for it are as different as the philosophies or religious beliefs on which the practice is based.

There is, however, a third field of comparison, which, in the depth of our being, justifies and explains the generality of experience which we mentioned at the outset. All monks are, in fact, in one way or another, searchers for the Absolute, the Infinite, the Ocean of Peace. The ways of approach are different; so also are the ways of conceiving and expressing the goal. But those who have tried to gain this experience – and who have made a close study of the sages of the diverse religions – are almost unanimous in affirming that the profound Reality sought by all is that which Christians call 'God'. The diversity of their ways of seeking is also an invitation to Christians to deepen their own faith.

It now remains for me to thank, once more, those who have contributed to the first version of this history, and also those who have helped me in the additions which appear in the present volume: Fr P. de Béthune, O.S.B., for 'Zen'; Frs F. Tiso and B. de Give, O.C.S.O., for 'Tibetan Monachism'. Finally, my thanks go to my confrère, Fr Adalbert de Vogüé, O.S.B., for the general revision of the text. The collaboration of these specialists gives to this small book a note of scientific research.

Part One

Born Before Christ:

Monastic Life in the East

CHAPTER 1

Hindu Monasticism

PRIMITIVE MONACHISM (2500–800 B.C.)

As far back as one can search into the history of religion in India, one finds men who are specialized in the practice of asceticism, the originators of different paths leading to the Absolute which later on would be followed by the people.

The hermits of the forests

Under a seal belonging to the Indus Valley Civilisation (2500–1500 B.C.) a figurine has been found representing a primitive god Shiva, seated in the yoga posture. This is evidence of the probable existence of ascetics even in those early days. It can legitimately be said therefore that India was one of the first to know and practise this way of life. The genesis and further developments of monastic life in India can be traced, thanks to the sacred writings of this country.

The oldest Scriptures, the *Vedas*, show that the first features of the existence of monastic life were connected with the social set up of the time. Society was then divided into four castes, namely: the priestly caste of the Brahmins, the caste of the Warriors, the caste of the Merchants and that of the Servants,[1] whose collaboration ensured the well-being of all. Many of these men gifted with a deep religious sense, were impressed by the order of the universe, and some among them, especially the 'seers' (*rishis*), strove for centuries to discover its principle. They attributed the origin of this order to divine beings, who like men on earth, belonged to four different groups and whose harmony among themselves and good relationship with men were sustained by placating them through sacrifices regularly offered in their honour. But the Vedas in which the *rishis* put their spiritual and poetic inspirations, show also that men craved for union with the divine principle of order. They realized that it required a special purification to prepare men to attain happiness after death. They were thus led to divide human life into several stages: Discipleship, Marriage, Retirement. When a boy no longer needed the care of his mother he was entrusted to a teacher who taught him his duties towards gods and men. Then he married and had to fulfil his obligations towards society. But the Law of Manu adds:

> When a householder sees wrinkles on his skin and his hairs turn grey, and looks at the son of his son, he should retire into the forest ... entrusting his wife to his son, or taking her with him.[2]

The best families entrusted the education of their sons to these religious men, and the boys lived a kind of monastic life with their Masters in the forest for several years. It is described in concise terms in the *Law of Manu*. The day began and ended with the prayer *gayatri*,[3] a hymn to the sun, image of God:

> At dawn let him stand, reciting quietly the *gayatri*, and at sunset let him recite it sitting till the time when the stars are clearly seen.[4]

The daily life was severe, for they believed that through 'rigour of the austerities' (*tapas*) they were sharing in the divine creative power. So the disciple was expected to keep silence as a rule:

> Not speaking before questions were asked him, living in the world as a dumb man[5]... Keeping the sacred fire burning, begging his food (in the nearby village) using

only a low bed and pleasing his Master.[6]

The laws of good behaviour, and above all Scripture, were the main topics he had to learn from his Master:

> When the time comes for study the young man makes an ablution according to the law, looking towards the North, and bows respectfully to the Holy Book... When beginning and ending the reading of the *Veda*, let him touch with respect the feet of his Master; let him read with folded hands for such is the homage due to Scripture.[7]

Then comes the explanation given by the Master (*Guru*). When listening to it the novice:

> Mastering his body, his voice, his senses and his mind, keeps his hands folded and his eyes set on his *guru*.[8]

Along with the external discipline of respect and obedience to the Master there was an interior effort of self-mastery fostered by studies:

> When yielding to the inclinations of the senses to lust, one cannot escape sin, but by mastering them one reaches supreme happiness... The senses can be controlled not only by starving them of their objects, but indeed by a steadfast study of the Sacred Sciences.[9]

Besides the studies, yogic meditation had an important place in the daily schedule:

> Alone in the forest, close to clean water, mastering his senses, let him repeat the *gayatri* with perfect recollection.[10]

Thus, under his Master's guidance the disciple improves on the fulfilment of his duties which lead him to 'eternal bliss'.[11] But the Master himself ought to give an example of joy, kindness and humility.

Any teaching having good as its object, should be given
without ill-treating the disciples, and let the Master who
wants to be fair use kind and pleasant words... He
should never be in a bad mood. Let him fear any worldly
honour as if it were poison.[12]

The hermits of the forest, living with their disciples in
ashrams, started a form of monastic life which still exists,
and this was akin to the way of life of the Desert Fathers. It
was the basis of Hindu monachism and had a great influence in the past. The *Upanishads*, sacred books
complementing the *Vedas*,[13] hand over to us the fruit of the
meditations of these early *gurus*, and the great epics like
Mahâbâratha and *Râmâyana* show the fame of their
wisdom, great enough to incite kings to go and seek their
advice.

Many young men renounced the world and dedicated
themselves to the search for eternal bliss under the guidance
of their *gurus*. Nevertheless *ashram* life was often considered to be only a stage towards final liberation. Many
ascetics wanted to rid themselves of all that was opposed to
divine nature and hoped to attain this through the practice
of more rigorous penances. Thus they began to leave their
ashrams and, according to Manu:

> Through always stricter austerities let them dry up their
> natural substance ... For them there is no more house or
> cooking, let them live on fruits or vegetable roots,
> keeping silence for ever.[14]

Finally when the ascetic feels that his end is coming:

> Let him walk towards the invincible region of the North
> East and proceed steadfastly up to the dissolution of the
> body, craving for divine union and living only on air and
> water.[15]

All these practices were originally meant for the three upper
castes, but gradually a legalistic trend developed giving the
Brahmin caste the monopoly of *ashram* life and sacrifices.

At the same time the wise men of the *Upanishads* continued their search for the origin and governing principle of the universe. They discovered that the Supreme Reality is an Infinite being which is beyond matter. The famous lines of *Brihad Upanishad* show well this direction of thought:

> From the unreal lead me to the real
> From darkness lead me to light
> From death lead me to immortality.[16] (*Brihad* 1, 3, 28)

Men in quest of the Absolute will therefore strive to free themselves from the created world, and from the sacrifices which are believed to maintain it. In their quest for union with the Infinite they introduced other types of monastic life.

New types of ascetics independent of the caste system

For these men, sacrifice was the spiritual fruit of penance and unworldiness. This way was open to all without distinction of caste or sex. It broke with organized society and developed the way of life of the ascetics leaving their ashrams for a wandering life. The *Upanishads* describe them as 'those who go forward' (*parivrajaka*), the 'renouncers' (*sannyâsi*), the mendicants (*bhiksu*).[17] Their search followed different ways more specialized than those of the previous period. One of them concentrates on meditation. The ascetic strives to dive beneath the material world and reach 'the other side' where the true realities exist. He repeats the sacred syllable *Aum* to ferry him across on his interior journey:

> He crosses over to the other side with the boat of the syllable *Aum* and lands in the interior space of the heart. But as the space within the heart gradually becomes manifest he enters carefully like a miner entering a mine in search of precious metal. Then let him enter the hall of *Brahman* ... and stand pure, purified, empty and tranquil, breathless, selfless, endless, indefectible, stable, eternal, unborn, independent, abiding in his own magnificence.[18]

Having thus shared in the magnificence of the Infinite he is certain to be united with it after death without further purification through rebirth.[19]

The wandering ascetics followed another way laying the stress on the 'rigour of the austerities'. The *Jâbâla Upanishad* gives a detailed description of their daily life:

Unencumbered as at birth, without any bounds or possessions, they set foot resolutely on the path of *Brahman*. With a clean mind, for the sake of maintaining life, they go out for alms at fixed times, with no other vessel than their stomachs, maintaining equanimity whether they get something or not. They may live in places such as a deserted house, a temple, a shrub or an anthill, the root of a tree or a potter's house, a fireplace or a sandbank in a river, a hill, a cave, the hollow of a tree, a stream or a deserted place. Without self-sense, without urges and effort, intent on meditation, established in the self, keen in removing evil deeds, they give up their bodies by renunciation.[20]

The two kinds of life, however were not sharply divided. A man could pass from one to another, and they were sometimes even regarded as successive stages on the path of asceticism. The essential thing was to realize that the Self, the *Brahman*, is also both the sustaining principle of all beings and the root of the personal self (*Atman*):[21]

Brahman is the universe, the supreme joy, the self-existent.[22]

This knowledge:

transcends hunger and thirst, sorrow and delusion, old age and death. The sage who has come to know this Self overcomes the desire for sons, the desire for riches and for worlds, and he sets forth on the life of a mendicant... Therefore, having done with learning, he desires to live as a child. When he has gone beyond both the state of childhood and learning, then he becomes a silent meditator (*muni*). Only when he has done with meditative and non-meditative states, does he become truly a *Brahmana* (Knower of *Brahman*).[23]

Another feature, one that seemed common to the different groups, was the use of yoga. We have seen it practised since the earliest times; it remained for all a means of self-mastery and concentration on the Absolute:

> In a solitary place, seating oneself in a relaxed posture, with a pure heart, neck and body straight, controlling all the senses ... meditating on the lotus of the heart, free from passions and pure, in the centre of which is the pure, the inconceivable, the sorrowless, the unmanifest, of eternal form the blissful, the peaceful, the immortal, the source of *Brahmâ*, Him who is without beginning, middle or end, one and all-pervading wisdom and bliss, formless and wonderful ... by meditating on Him the sage reaches the source of being, the witness of all, who is beyond all darkness.[24]

THE FIRST ORGANIZED GROUPS
(800 B.C.–100 A.D.)

Unfortunately, the wonderful teaching of the Upanishads remained in the hands of small groups of disciples; and for the people, the austerities practised by the ascetics formed a barrier just as insurmountable as that of caste. Religious souls, searching for a way to the Divine that would be within their scope, were unsatisfied and so provided the ground for secondary religious currents that ran parallel to the main streams. The political barriers of the North of India, divided at that period into small coexisting kingdoms, also favoured this development in diverse directions, soon to manifest itself in the different schools of Hinduism and Buddhism.

The Jains (VIII cent. B.C.)

One of the first sects to emerge from the shadows is Jainism. Its origin is unknown but it enters history about 800 B.C. with Parshva, a prince of Benares turned monk. In the Jain tradition, however, he was only the twenty-third of the *Tirthankaras* or prophets 'those who show the way'. The twenty-fourth and last was to be Mahavira Jina, another prince, hailing from Bihar, who appeared two hundred years later. From him stems the real beginning of the new religion. The success of Mahavira was considerable. The precise rules according to which he organized monastic life, are still followed today. By the time of his death in about 468 B.C. thousands of men and women kings and princesses, had forsaken all to become monks and *Sâdhvîs*[25] (women ascetics), or had striven, to a greater or lesser degree, to become fervent lay people trying, according to their state in life, to imitate the law of the perfect.

Jainism was truly open to all, irrespective of caste or sex. The forms of worship were simple and expressed in the ordinary language of the people. It followed a line somewhat similar to the *Upanishads*, but without recognizing the existence of a supreme Being. The creed affirmed the superiority of the spiritual by sacrifice that was wholly interior, by detachment and by non-violence, while at the same time striving with intense fervour to liberate the soul from its human condition, dominated by time.

In Jain teaching, the unique reality is the Universe, which exists from all eternity and does not need a creator. It is, however, composed of two elements, one spiritual and living, *Jiva*, the soul, the other material and not living, *ajîva*. Every person has a spiritual soul in which perception is more or less obscured by the effects of preceding actions, *karma*, which cover it as with a layer of dust. All man's effort must tend therefore towards ridding himself of this obscuring substance, 'burning' it by sustained asceticism in order to reach the blessed state of *siddha* (omniscience), a state of total liberation in which the soul acquires knowledge transcending that of the senses, and enjoy infinite happiness and power. It has entered into the fullness of being.

The attainment of this liberation postulates the practice of the 'three jewels': – Right Vision, Right Knowledge, Right Conduct; that is, one must recognize true reality, adhere to it in spirit, and model one's life upon it. The conduct of the perfect is essentially dominated by respect for life and by non-violence. It is strengthened by the 'great vows': the renunciation of taking the life of any living thing, lying, theft, all sexual acts and attachment to material things. The last is to be practised chiefly by a life of continual pilgrimage, the ascetic begging for his food and using only the minimum of clothing. Four great virtues help him to carry out his vows: universal friendship, seeing the good side of others and rejoicing in it, universal compassion, and tolerance of evil-doers. For almost two thousand years the Jain tradition survived in India; it had its brilliant periods (the fifth to the thirteenth centuries of our era), and its declines. But even today, their ascetics or group of *sâdhvis* are to be seen on the roads, silent and reserved, visiting and comforting the communities of the faithful who, in return for instruction, provide for their slender needs.

The Buddha and the first devotees of Shiva (V cent. B.C.)

Though the movements inaugurated by the *Upanishads* and by Jainism were important, it seems that by about the fifth century B.C. they had still reached only restricted circles of the population. The mass of religious people remained unsatisfied with the ritualistic domination of the Brahmins and the extreme asceticism preached by the wandering monks. Thus during the very life of Mahavira, we find another prince of the Ganges region, belonging to the Gautama family, abandoning everything to find a solution to the problem of suffering in the world. He was recognized as the 'Buddha' the 'enlightened one', and he was to propagate the teaching that bears his name, a teaching all the more successful, because it offered a kind of middle way, easier and more acceptable. We shall deal later with the development of Buddhist monasticism; here it is sufficient to notice the point whence this new shoot on the trunk of a Hinduism already almost a thousand years old sprang, whose multiform growth we must continue to consider.

The Absolute, already shown by the *Upanishads* as attracting men by the light and happiness that emanated from it, now began to be seen as having an interest in mankind, arousing a response of love, which was to lend a new colour to certain forms of Hindu monasticism.

From the Vedic age we have hymns praising the goodness of *Rudra-Shiva*, but one of the latest *Upanishads* gives a clear conception of grace, in its recognition of the highest forms of contemplation, as a gift from God.[26] Meanwhile, Jains and Buddhists had developed devotion to the saints of their religions, an attitude of imitation and reverence towards these benevolent intermediaries between men and the Infinite. The stories of the *Râmâyana* and *Mahâbhârata* immortalize Hindu heroes and show them as having frequent intercourse with the gods. About second century B.C. devotion to *Shiva* had become so strong that some ascetics occupied their whole lives with it; these were the *Pâshupatas*. In the face of ritualism and asceticism, a new way was opened, that of the gift of self out of love for a personal god. This spiritual concept gained ground widely during the following centuries under the name of *Bhakti*.

Nevertheless all the problems were not completely solved. Orthodox Hinduism felt its very existence menaced by the divergences of these spiritual movements and devotions. Moreover, the ascetics continued, in some way to reserve for themselves the monopoly of salvation. They alone were certain to attain it. Even in the least exclusive movements of the time, such as Jainism and Buddhism, one had to die in the monastic state to escape the wheel of reincarnation. Then again, the better elements in society were tempted to leave traditional orthodoxy and their social duties to consecrate themselves in solitude to what they believed to be the way of salvation.

The book Bhagavad Gîta: a reaction both secular and mystic (200 B.C.)

It was the genius of the author of the *Bhagavad Gîta* to

incorporate the dynamism of these diverse elements into the body of traditional Hinduism. Unlike Buddha and Jina, the author advocated, for the devotion of the masses, *Krishna*, the man-god, a kind of incarnation (*avatar*) of the Supreme God. This new theological perspective led him to a radical change in the understanding of salvation which prevailed up to his time. In all the previous religious currents worldly activities were centred on man: through his actions, the fruits of his desires, he became tainted by or fettered with matter, and was thus bound by a succession of rebirths. The only means of liberation were the purification from matter through the suppression of desire and even withdrawal from all activities.[27]

The author of the Gîtâ shows, on the contrary, that all human actions have their source and model in the transcendent and totally unselfish action of God. Man will obtain salvation by conforming his actions to God's ways:

Works do not taint me. I have no yearning for the fruits of work.
He who thus knows me is not bound (to rebirth) by actions.[28]

Persevering efforts towards self-mastery are obviously needed to reach that perfect tuning in with God. Their first aim will be to keep under control the two mainsprings of our passions, namely lust and anger. For that purpose one has to overcome them in the senses, mind and intellect, where they usually lurk:

Senses, mind and intellect are the places where they lurk; through these they smother wisdom... Therefore restrain the senses first... Then control your mind, restrain your imagination, hold thought well in check. Thus become unflickering like a lamp standing in a windless place. Thirdly, be controlled by the intellect.[29]

This self-control allows a man to act like God in an unselfish way, seeking only the universal good:

Let not your motive be the fruit of works, nor your
attachment be to inaction... When a man has cast off
attachment to the fruits of works, ever content, depending on none, though he engages in work, in fact he does
not work at all.[30]

Hence the well known rule:

He who sees inaction in action and action in inaction, he
is wise among men, he is a yogi.[31]

This total detachment may look impossible, even inhuman.
And it would be so if the *Gîtâ* did not point out another
dimension of man's action, namely its connection with love
for God:

The object of the senses turns away from the soul who
ceases to feed on them, but the taste for them remains...
Even this taste fades away when the Supreme is seen...
How easily I am won by him who bears me in mind
unceasingly, thinking of nothing else.[32]

Selfish desires and passions can be transcended by a higher
and stronger love for the Lord who invites man to trust in
Him, offering Him all his actions

Whatever you do, whatever you eat, whatever you offer
in sacrifice or give away in alms, whatever penance you
may perform, offer it up to me.[33]

Conversely this constant communion with God's love transforms all human actions into sacrifice and worship. Indeed
all are done as a response to the inspiration of the Inner
Ruler and thus they become a homage to the Absolute
present in the heart of men. This sacrificial dimension given
to unselfish fulfilment of man's duties takes the place of
ascesis and sacrifice in the hierarchy of the means of salvation. Secular activities are thus reconciled with a total
self-surrender to the Absolute and a way towards God is
open to all men of good will.

Taking also into account the diversity of men's characters, the new way is made of four branches henceforward traditional in Hinduism: *Jnâna Mârga*, the way of knowledge through wisdom and philosophic reflection, *Bhakti Mârga*, the way of love and devotion, *Yoga Mârga*, the way of methodical concentration and *Karma Mârga*, the way of action or carrying out duty with detachment. Each of these ways (*Mârga*) leads to union with *Brahmâ* through the stripping of the self.

In reaction against monastic exclusiveness, which reserved salvation for its own members, the *Gîtâ* thus offered it to every man according to his state, through the accomplishment of duty and union with God:

> They who in peace from passion, fears and anger, inhere in me, making me their sanctuary, they come to share in the manner of my being... In any way that men approach me, in that way do I return their love.[34]

The following chants make clear the superiority of the *dharma*, the 'discipline of action', in the fulfilment of the duties of one's caste, over the way of renunciation:

> Both renunciation and performing work are paths to the Supreme, but of the two, to engage in the yoga of work is better than surrender of work.[35]

One can, therefore, say that in many respects the *Bhagavad Gîtâ* is an anti-monastic text, putting the ideal of the carrying out of duty with love and disinterestedness before ascetic renunciation. But it expressed also a healthy reaction, pointing out that true perfection is not found in the fulfilment of observances but in purity of heart:

> He who does the work that he is to do, yet covets not its fruits, he is a *sannyasi*, he is a *yogi*.[36]

This attitude leads finally to a better understanding of monachism. It no longer appears as an exclusive means of salvation, but as a vocation among others, one which highlights the qualities of self-mastery and concentration on the Absolute which are essential elements of any human life.[37] Being anxious to keep all the traditional values, the author of the *Gîtâ* seems to adopt this view. Indeed he does not want to suppress monachism and he considers as efficient means of perfection 'the safeguard of the vow of celibacy' 'a life spent in solitude' and even 'in silence and without fixed abode'.[38]

In practice this dichotomy was resolved in two ways: first of all each of the three chief ways, *jnâna, bhakti,* and *yoga,* found its fulfilment in a particular form of monastic life. Secondly, men were allowed to quit any of the four traditional stages of life in order to become renouncers:

> After completing the life of a student, let him become a householder. After completing the life of a householder, let him become a forest dweller. After completing the life of a forest dweller, let him renounce all things, otherwise let him renounce even the state of student or the state of a householder.[39]

The attempts at a synthesis made by the *Bhagavad Gîtâ* had thus the effect of integrating more deeply the caste ethic with the monastic ideal of self-mastery and search for the Absolute. Monotheism gave also to monachism a new and deep theological perspective and, purified by right criticism, it would draw fresh vigour from devotion to a personal God.

GENESIS OF THE PRESENT MONASTIC CURRENTS (II–XVIII CENT. A.D.)

The centuries that followed the *Bhagavad Gîtâ* witnessed the organisation of philosophic thought in India into systems (*dharsanas*),[40] while devotion to personal forms of the deity developed, which, in their turn, were to influence the philosophers. The forms taken by monastic life during this period reflect the society of the time and its religious concepts. Two principal divinities, *Shiva* and *Vishnu*, drew the devotion of the faithful. The *Shaivas* were the first to possess a definite monastic organisation, perhaps under the influence of Buddhist monks or in competition with them.

(a) Shaiva ascetics

The 'Pâshupatas'

In the second century of our era, Lakulisha, a famous *guru*, wrote rules of spiritual life for the *Pâshupatas* ascetics which were expounded during the following centuries by the most famous masters of the sect.[41] They regard *Shiva-Pashupati* as the Absolute, the origin of all, transcending the world by contemplation, but sustaining it by his power, *Shakti* – often conceived as a female deity – and finally drawing all men to himself by his grace and love. All human beings remain animal (*pashu*) as long as bonds attach them to the world of senses. These bonds are really actions inspired by self-interest, knowledge limited to the senses, sufferings and pleasures which make them ignorant and finite beings. They remain in this state until *Shiva* unites them to himself by his grace and becomes their Lord (*pati*).

This transformation, attained by Lakulîsha, and given by him to his disciple, Kushika, is transmitted in an uninterrupted chain from *gurus* to disciples. It is a tradition in the strict sense, direct and personal, of a saving experience of union with God. It consists in the realisation by the disciple of the divine presence in the *guru*, through which the initiated one gains access to the divine world and to intimate union with Shiva. He can then, in this turn, become a master and transmit the experience to others.

The disciple was prepared for this realization in several stages, often marked by a ceremony of partial initiation, (*dîksâ*) the rites of which grew more elaborate as time went on. There was first a period of probation before the reception of the *mantra*,[42] the habit,[43] and the regular practice of monastic life, with its non-violence, celibacy, self-mastery, frankness, withdrawal from the world, gentleness, service of the *guru* and restriction to food obtained by begging. For the practice of this asceticism, the guru arranged an environment that would best sustain the novice in his efforts.

Once inured to hardship, the disciple went on to the second stage which took place in the world. He had then to conceal his status of monk and, by acting stupidly, make people despise him. Thus did he reject pride of caste and learn to put complete trust in *Shiva*. The joy of union with him enabled the monk to master all suffering. He was then ready for the third stage, six months of intensive yoga, practised in the solitude of a cave or a deserted house. This effort led to perfect patience and unbroken contemplation. He passed the rest of his life in isolated spots such as the burning places of the dead, where he subsisted on occasional and unsolicited gifts, completely absorbed in *Shiva* and waiting only for the liberation of death to be united to him through love, for the *Pâshupata* follows essentially a way of *bhakti*.

Such was the ideal of Shaivism as described in its books at the period when Christian monachism was born and began to expand. But for a better understanding of the subject, it seems useful to add a few notes on subsequent developments in Hindu monachism.

First we must not forget that, apart from the more or less organised movements, there were still ascetics living freely. In the bhakti Shaivite tradition, they were to produce mystics and poets of a high order, such as the sixty-three 'saints' (*Nâyanars* or *Adiyars*) of the Tamilnad, whose chants, full of the love of God and confidence in his grace, nourish popular piety even at the present day.

The monastic order of Shankara VIIIth century A.D.

In the eighth century Shankara, the great teacher of the *Advaita*,[44] was also the first to endow Hindu monachism with a firm organization by founding a religious order. His monasteries were established throughout India as fortresses of orthodoxy. The monks devoted themselves primarily to study, putting the way of *Jnâna*, that is, of knowledge and wisdom above all others. They brought to its height the school of *Vedanta*, which recognizes the uniqueness of the

Absolute and his presence in the heart of each being, an idea that has dominated the thought of India to our own day and, in a way, defined its orthodoxy. Their spiritual path was the realization of this presence at its source in the self and the immersion of the whole being in it:

> The immutable which is the beginning of all beings and the reality behind the universe, that in which the perfected ever repose.[45]

In the centuries that followed, the order founded by Shankara split into several branches of which the most important were recruited exclusively from the Brahmin caste. In former times, a kind of military order was attached to each monastery to protect the faithful against the Muslims or rival Hindu sects. Actually the monasteries or *maths* were in the nature of spiritual centres towards which gravitated numbers of layfolk, who had a monk as guru.

Shaiva Siddhanta IXth century A.D.

Against this teaching of the Advaita there arose in the south of India a pietist reaction, the *Shaiva Siddhânta*. Beginning from the ninth century, certain of its ascetics were to form monastic groups in which the practices were essentially yogic or tantric.[46] Later on they were to reassume the structures of the *Pashupatas*, but insisting on elaborate initiation rites and on the development of spiritual energies by the correct recital of the *mantras* and of the fundamental sound *Aum*. (They had also a special initiation for the consecration of spiritual masters or *âchâryas*). Some of these masters sometimes became counsellors to the kings and princes who ruled the feudal states that grew up from the sixth to the thirteenth century. They received endowments, lived with groups of disciples in the *maths* and were charged with the administration of temples, sometimes important ones. Wealth proved their undoing; it led to the abandonment of celibacy and the disappearance of many of the *maths*.

Virashaivism, IXth century and other Shaivist groups

In many cases, the *Shaiva Siddhântas* were replaced by ascetics of a new sect, *Virashaivism* or *Lingayatism*,[47] which represent, from the Christian point of view, one of the most interesting realizations of Hindu monachism. Founded in the eleventh century by Basava, a Brahmin minister at the court of a Jain prince in central India, it formed a new reaction against the abuses of ritualism and the caste system. It preached the equality of all men because of the divine presence existing in each of them, the dignity of work, and an essentially interior worship. Profiting from the experience of Buddhists and Jains, its monachism was well organized. It included resident monks, living in the *maths* under a superior, and itinerant preachers returning at regular intervals to the monastery. Unfortunately the sect finished up by itself becoming a caste. A certain spiritual renewal, however, among the *Lingayat* monks has taken place in our own times.

We must take note also of other groups of *Shaivas*, at the beginning of the tenth century, specializing in a yoga often mingled with tantrism and sometimes degenerating into magic and moral perversion.

The current of Shaivistic mysticism continues in our age. Its chief feature remains love of God, expressed by a total surrender of the self to *Shiva*, and finding expression in hymns, ancient but still in use, as is this of the *Tirumular*:

> The one who says that *Shiva* and love are two
> verily knows nothing.
> Who will ever understand?
> What is *Shiva* and what is love?
> Only he who has discovered that
> *Shiva* is love and love is *Shiva*,
> attains to the peace.
> one forever with *Shiva*-the-love.[48]

(b) Vishnuite ascetics

The first mystic Vth century A.D.

Parallel with the *Shaivists* and developing on similar lines, the *Vaishnavas* also had their groups of ascetics, but they began later. The first that can be identified are the *Alvars* of Tamilnad, groups of mystic poets, taking shape from the fifth to the ninth century and approximating to the *Nayanar Shaivists*. A theological school, closely resembling that of *Shankara*, and recognizing monastic branches parallel with its own, appeared with *Râmânuja* (eleventh century). Nimbârka (twelfth century), and *Madhva* (thirteenth century). Each had its monasteries, centres of doctrinal propaganda, its military order to protect it and, at the present time its *maths*, spiritual centres exercising influence over specific bodies of lay people.

Krishna and Rama devotees XIII–XVIIIth century A.D.

With the progress of the Muslim kingdoms in India other groups appeared, belonging to movements influenced by Islam or in reaction against it. From the thirteenth century to the eighteenth, but particularly in the fifteenth, cults centred on the *Avatars* of *Vishnu*, *Krishna* and *Rama* flourished. The founders were often ascetics gifted in mysticism and poetry. They appeared in all parts of India; *Vallabha*, originating in the south, (Telegu), *Caitanya* in Bengal and *Râmanânda* and *Kabîr* in the north. All these lived in the fifteenth century but, thanks to their writings in the vernacular language and to the monastic groups they founded, their influence is still felt in our own days. They taught how to approach God by a progressive purification of love. Beginning with the prayer of petition, the devotee lifts himself to a higher moral level, to goodwill towards others and to the praise of God. Then he is caught up by the grace of the Lord, who purifies him from all attachment, establishes him in his love, in peace and in spiritual joy. He still suffers from the separation imposed by the body, but aspires to total union after death.[49]

MODERN MONASTICISM

At the beginning of the eighteenth century, Western ideas began to exert a stronger influence. Hinduism absorbed certain elements from Christianity but at the same time reacted to it, realizing its own values. A renewal of vitality pervaded Hindu monachism in general. One of the most remarkable innovations was the foundation by Vivekananda of the *Rāmakrishna Mission*, a monastic order whose organization was inspired by Catholic missionary congregations. But, in the traditional line of the great gurus, there arose also an important number of new *ashrams*, founded by spiritual masters of all trends. They trained their disciples in religious experiences some of which were undoubtedly profound, and several of their institutions exerted an influence that now extends well beyond the frontiers of India. Among the most famous may be mentioned the Ashrams founded by *Rāmana Mahârshi Tiruvannamalai*, by *Aurobindo* at Pondicherry by *Narayana* in Kerala and by *Shivananda* near Rishikesh. Noteworthy also, both in the social and religious order are the *Ashrams* or groups which claim as their founder *Mahatma Gandhi* or his disciple, *Vinobâ Bhave*. The thousands of young people who come to India each year to visit these *Ashrams* bear witness to their strong attraction as spiritual centres and to the world's need of the values they represent.

It is impossible to evaluate in a few lines a monastic tradition going back for three thousand years. It seems, however, that in spite of inevitable errors and deviations, often due to men's infidelity to their ideals, there can be discerned, through the various forms of life and thought, some very definite common characteristics.

The most striking feature of Hindu monachism is perhaps the emphasis it puts on 'realization', the actual experience of union with the Absolute.

This union is considered as the essential goal of man's quest; it is sometimes conceived as an immersion of the self in the interior presence, sometimes as a loving relationship with a personal God. Equally diverse are the ways that lead to it, knowing the joy of the divine favour as well as the darkness of the mystery surrounding the Infinite. All, however, insist on the necessity of asceticism and direction by a spiritual master in order that one may commit oneself entirely to the pursuit of the Absolute. Finally, this spiritual effort implies generosity in the giving of self, an ardent desire for the goal to be attained and techniques of asceticism and prayer which can provide for all a source of inspiration and holy emulation.

India, in fact, seems to have been the cradle of monastic life in the world. Almost all branches of Hinduism admit of a form of monachism, and it is from the plains of the Ganges that Buddhism arose with its thousands of monks spread throughout all Asia and beyond.

In the first centuries of our era, Indian *gurus* used to travel to the West, as they do still in our own times. Clement of Alexandria makes careful note of their different categories: – the ascetics of the forests, the Brahmins, the 'gymnophists' (Jains) and the Buddhists. In Syria, the gateway to India from the West, the earliest Christian ascetics carried out practices which seem to call to mind the observances of the Hindu *Sannyâsis*, living as mendicant pilgrims and performing extreme penances. But there is no proof of any direct influence from the religions of Asia on Christian monachism and it seems, besides, that the latter sprang spontaneously from the Gospels. The similarities thus bear witness to man's fundamental desire to surrender himself completely to the search for the Absolute.

Hindu monks belonging to the *Bhakti* current crave for union by love with a personal God. The monastic orders of the *Advaita* tend to strive for the realization of their identification with the Absolute considered as the source of all beings. The Jain by persevering detachment struggle for the full liberation through which the soul realizes its godhood. It is by way of interior emptiness that the Buddhists strive to achieve immersion in the Ocean of Peace; nevertheless their monachism admits of many different branches which we are now going to study, for they often present suggestive comparisons with Christianity.

Notes

1   The traditional names of the castes are: *Kshatrias* for the warriors, *Vaisyas* for the merchants and *Sudras* for the servants. Besides these were the out-castes whom Ghandi called the *Harijans* (people of God Hari).

2   *Law of Manu* VI. 8. It is a compilation made in the beginning of the Christian era, but composed of texts sometimes very ancient. They give the name of *Brahamachari* to the celibate student, that of *Griastha* to the householder, of *Vanaprastha* to those who retire in the forest. Nowadays young men preparing for religious life are still called *Brahamachari* and elderly people retiring for a life of prayer *Vanaprastha*.

3   Literal translation of the text of the Gayatri:
    'Let us meditate on (lit. put on) the adorable brilliance of God the Saviour that he may impel our thoughts'
    Before reciting this prayer people used to say in a drawn out way the sacred syllable *Aum*, a summary of God's name expressing and manifesting his presence; they added the words 'Bhuh, Bhuvah, Swar', meaning 'earth, air, heavens', considered as the three levels of the world animated by the rising sun. Thousands of Hindus today recite these prayers in the same way.

4   *Law of Manu II.* 102.

5   Ibid. II, 110.

6   Ibid. II, 108.

7   Ibid. II, 70–71.

8   Ibid. II, 92.

9   Ibid. II, 93, 96.

10 Ibid. II, 104.

11 Ibid. VI, 84. These notions of truth (*Satya*), eternal law (*Rita*), self-dedication (*dîksä*) are very ancient and still remain the fundamental ideas of the present monastic life in India. That of *tapas* (rigour of austerities giving men a sharing in the creative power) is found in the later parts of the *Rig Veda* (one of the *Vedas* books) about 1000 B.C.; but it was mainly developed in the *Upanishads*.

12 *Law of Manu*, II, 159; 161; 162.

13 The *Upanishads* complete and develop the texts of the *vedas*, sometimes by a series of reflections, sometimes by illustrative fables. The principal *Upanishads* were composed between 800 and 300 B.C.; the *Aranyakas Upanishads* describe in detail the life in the *ashrams*.

14 *Law of Manu* VI, 25.

15 Ibid. VI, 31.

16 On the development of Indian ideas on asceticism see: 'The origin of asceticism and of the Ashrama Dharma' in *Bharati Bulletin of Indology*, Benares Hindu University, VIII, 1964–1965, pp. 1–26; Van Troy, 'Early Shiva ascetic movements', *All Asia Monastic Meeting 1973*; F. Acharya, 'Le monachisme en Inde' in *Collectanea* 1967, No. 3; R.V. De Smet, 'The Status of Scriptures in the Holy History of

India' in *Research Seminar on non-Biblical Scriptures.* Bangalore 1975.

17 The type of wandering monk, the 'renouncer' is described chiefly in *Brihadâranyaka Upanishad* 3, 5, 1 and 4, 4, 22, and in *Mundaka Upanishad* 1, 2, 11. In these excerpts and in the following ones, we have used the translations of R.O. Zaehner in *Hindu Scriptures*, of S Radhakrishnan in *The Principal Upanishads*, of R. Panikkar in 'The Monk according to the Indian Sacred Scriptures', in *All Asia Monastic Meeting 1973*, of Juan Mascaro in *The Bhagavad Gita*, without, however, reproducing any of them literally.

18 *Maîtrí Up.* VI, 28.

19 Hindus generally believe that man has to be purified through several rebirths before attaining complete union with the Absolute.

20 *Jâbâla Up.* 6.

21 *Brihad. Up.* 1, 3, 28. The discovery of the 'Self', of the Absolute, not only as present in the heart of man, but as the source of the good existing in every creature is presented in a moving fashion in the *Brihadâranyaka Upanishad* by a dialogue between Yajnavalkya and his wife Maitreyi, whom he wants to leave to go into solitude in order to devote himself to the search of the Absolute:

Verily it is not for the love of the husband that the husband is dear, but a husband is dear for the love of the Self. Verily it is not for the love of the wife that the wife is dear, but a wife is dear for the love of the Self... Verily it is not for the love of all that all is dear, but all are dear for the love of the Self. Verily, O Maitreyi, it is the Self that should be seen, heard, reflected on and deeply pondered. Verily by seeing the Self and hearing it, by thinking of it and knowing it, all is known. (2, 4, 5) In the space within the heart lies the controller of all, the Lord of all, the ruler of all... Him the Brahmin strive to know by the study of the *Vedas* by sacrifices, by giving alms, by penance, by fasting. Once a man has come to know him, he becomes a 'silent sage' (*muni*). Desiring him alone as their world, monks leave their homes ... to lead a beggar's life (4, 4, 22).

22 *Mahânârayana Up.* 530.

23 *Brihadaranyaka Up.* 3, 5, 1.

24 *Kaivalya Up.* 5–7.

25 The solicitude for purification by detachment from matter, attested by Jain monachism presents many points in common with Platonic doctrine and suggests influences that would be interesting to study. For Jain monachism for women, see N. Shanta 'The Continual Pilgrimage in Christian monks and Asian Religions', *Cistercian Studies* IX, 1974, pp. 242 ss.

26 *Katha Up.* 1, 20, 23.

27 See R.V. De Smet, 'A Copernical reversal: the Gîtâkara's reformulation of Karma', in *Chinmoya Mission Silver Jubilee Volume*, Poona 1976, pp. 34–41. Most of our quotations from the Gîtâ are borrowed from this article. We shall quote the Bhagavad Gîtâ as B.G.

28 B.G. 4, 14.

29　Group citations: B.G. 3, 40–41; 6, 10–19; 2, 39, borrowed from R.V. De Smet loc. cit.

30　B.G. 2, 47; 4, 19–20.

31　Ibid. 4, 18.

32　Ibid. 2, 58, 61; 8, 14.

33　Ibid. 9, 27. Appeals of this kind are often repeated in the *Gîtâ*, for example: 2; 61; 6, 14; 7, 29; 8, 7; 8, 22; etc.

34　B.G. 4, 1–11; same idea in 6, 46.

35　Ibid. 5, 2.

36　Ibid. 6, 1.

37　See: R. Panikkar 'Problems of monastic aggiornamento' *in Monastic Studies*, Michaelmas 1969, p. 110.

38　B.G. 14; 6, 10; 17, 52; 12, 19.

39　*Jâbâla Up.* 4. This custom was probably in existence before the writing of the *Gîtâ*, which strengthened it and explained its true raison d'être.

40　Many of these systems do not admit the existence of a first cause, independent of the universe.

41　These basic texts are the *Pâshupatas Sutras* attributed to Lakulisha. They form a kind of memory aid for the *gurus* (spiritual masters) and they have been explained later in the *Panchârthabhâshya* (4th & 5th centuries), the *Ganakârikâ (7th century), and the Bhâshya* (10th century); see Van Troy art. cit.

42　A *mantra* is a short form of prayer presented at the initiation. It is sometimes the guru's own and he passes the same prayer to each disciple; sometimes it is chosen by the guru as being most appropriate to a disciple.

43　The habit sometimes consisted in the absence of clothing, some ascetics wearing scarcely a loin cloth as a sign of detachment. At the present time most of them wear a kind of ochre-coloured tunic (*kavi*) with a shawl of the same colour.

44　The teaching of the *Advaita* or 'non-dualism' considers the Absolute as the One to whom nothing can be added, who cannot be described and who is present in all that exists. Some disciples of Shankara were to develop his teaching in an uncompromising monism.

45　Shankara, *Direct Realisation* 113, in *Selected works of Shankarâchârya*, translated by S. Venkataramanam, Madras, 1944.

46　Tantrism: philosophic and religious schools often associated with a pantheistic worship in which special importance is given to the goddess-wife of the supreme god. Its philosophy contains lofty speculations but sometimes bordering on magic rites, with the practice of occultism and with obscenities.

47　Lingaitism comes from *linga* an oblong and black stone symbolising the divinity in which there is neither form nor colour. The linga is given at the time of the initiation and it is attached to the neck as a symbol of the divine presence. It is used also in meditation as an object of concentration, first exterior and then interiorised. The masters of this school describe the steps of spiritual ascent resembling that of Christian mysticism.

48 Quoted by Abhishiktananda in *Prayer*, p. 67, note 10.
49 See: McNicol, *The living religion of the Indian people*, p. 86 quoted by Gispert Sauch in his commentary of the *Narada Bhakti Sutra* (cyclostyled). We should also mention among the most famous mystics of this school, *Tulasidâs* and *Tukârâm*. In modern times we find an echo of the same inspiration in *R. Tagore.*

CHAPTER 2

Buddhist Monasticism

The Building up of the Institution

When Gautama the ascetic of the clan of Sakya, the *Sakyamuni*, became the Buddha, the 'Enlightened One', he set out to preach his doctrine, his *dharma*, and disciples joined him. He was then no different from the numerous wandering ascetics who, with a train of monks, their initiates, travelled the roads of India, discoursed in the towns and market places and held contests in oratory, much relished by the public.

The transformation of the *Sakyaputta Samanas* or ascetic disciples of *Sakyamuni*, into a monastic order that became the foundation of a religion embracing millions of followers, is for the student a religious phenomenon of the highest interest. The limits of this chapter do not allow us to consider it in all its details; it is equally impossible to give a complete survey of the teaching of the Buddha and the different schools that developed after him. We shall be content with trying to assess the role played by monastic life in Buddhism as we follow the development of those institutions which, right up to our own time, encourage monks in the pursuit of their ideal. It will be necessary also, in the course of our study, to take into account the interaction of ancient far-eastern cultures with the ideas propagated by the Buddha and show their repercussion on the ideal and practice of monastic life.

The region where the Buddha and his first disciples lived was subjected to the monsoon system, where the rains made it impossible to travel from June to September. These climatic conditions forced the ascetics to settle in one place for months at a time. They made use of these periods to regroup themselves and deepen their teaching.

As the numbers of Gautama's disciples increased and as, at the same time, they received gifts of parks and buildings, the best of their seasonal stopping places or *avasas* were gradually transformed into permanent residences. Their position had to conform to the demands of monastic life. In the book of rules, *Vinaya tipika*, we see King Bimbisara reflecting before offering a piece of ground to Buddha:

> Where shall I find a place suitable for the Blessed One to live? It must be neither too far from the town nor too near, so that one can come and go, easy of access for people who wish to see him, not too frequented during the day, and at night exposed to neither noise nor danger, far from unpleasant smells, hidden from men and suited to a life of retirement. (*Vinaya* I, 143)[1]

As the periods of living together were prolonged, rules were drawn up for the good order of the community and to favour spiritual research. Each rule was preceded by a recital describing a difficult situation as reported to Buddha, who then prescribed the right solution to the problem posed; whence the stereotyped phrase:

> When the Lord Buddha heard that, he said... In the *avasa* there were certain simple buildings for common use but most of the monks lived in isolated cells or *vihara* some distance apart from each other.

Following the custom of Hindu ascetics, the disciples of Sakyamuni met at the full and the new moon. At these monthly reunions, called *Uposatha*, they repeated the elements of their *dharma* and later a part of their rules. This recalling of the law led quite naturally to an examination of his life in which each monk accused himself of his faults. In the course of time the rules thus recited were formed into a definite code of about two hundred articles, the *Patimokkha*, and the reparation for offences became a rite of purification carried out before the recital of the sacred texts.

These community exercises gradually gave rise to groups each with its own special features and the monks identified themselves with the *avasa* to which they belonged. When these establishments multiplied, a territory was marked out for each, care being taken to leave an empty space between the boundaries of each *avasa*. This enabled the monks to go out to seek what they needed (whence their name of *bhikshus* or mendicants) without fear of conflict.

The eremitic or itinerant life in its origins continued parallel with the community life in the *avasa*. The hermits were regarded as leading a more saintly and austere life than the monks living close to towns.[2]

During his long life the Buddha remained the centre of unity for his disciples and each submitted to his decisions. But at the approach of death he refused to name a successor. He thus departed from the tradition of the hindu gurus and from the custom of dynastic succession practised in the kingdoms of the plain, preferring to give his followers the democratic organization that prevailed in the clans living at the foot of the Himalayas whence he had originated. With them all decisions were made in full assembly, following the pattern of ancestral custom. The Buddha, in the same manner, entrusted authority to the assembly of his disciples, the *sangha*, guided by his teaching, the *dharma*.

The reunions of each *avasa* or local *sangha* thus developed into a system of government. The formally constituted assembly had power of jurisdiction over its members; and its decisions, *sanghakammas*, or 'acts of the *sangha*', had the force of law for all the members. By degrees strict rules were formulated for the conduct of these gatherings. They fixed the smallest number, varying from four to twenty, necessary for each kind of business to be carried out. The right of participation in the assemblies was reserved to the resident members of the *avasa*, always on condition that they had not incurred the *parivasa* or sentence of temporary excommunication for a serious fault. The decisions to be taken were read and silence signified approbation; otherwise they were discussed and a vote was taken. If the discussion came to a deadlock, a commission could be appointed to clear the matter up.

At first the meetings were presided over by the oldest monk and were convened either by common agreement, for everyday matters, or in extraordinary session when there was a difference of opinion among the members on deciding a point under discussion. Later, under the pressure of kings and of the need for a good administration of the *sangha*, a superior was named to supervise the management of material business. As he presided over the meetings of the *sangha*, disciplinary measures also fell within his province.

This system makes the Buddhist regime of leadership and government very different from that of Hindu monachism, centred as it was, on the Spiritual Master, the guru, around whom disciples gathered. In Buddhism the community took first place, choosing a head for itself to ensure its progress. The Superior thus chosen had certainly more than a purely administrative authority for he was selected from among the old and experienced monks; but he was rarely the spiritual guide for the whole monastery.[3] In fact, each postulant chose for himself his Spiritual Master or *Upajjhaya* who, with the aid of an assistant, the *acharya*, had the duty of presenting his candidate for admission into the *sangha* and of assuring his formation. The period of probation, originally envisaged as ten years, is now sometimes reduced to a minimum of five years.

The Spiritual Quest

Such is the general framework in which the *bhikshu* has always evolved, but let us try to understand his interior quest and place it in its Buddhist setting. At the basis of Buddhist teaching lie the four 'Noble Truths', the *Arya Satya:*

> This, O monks, is the noble truth of sorrow: birth, old age, sickness and death; all this is sorrow ... This, O monks, is the noble truth of the cause of sorrow: desire. This, O monks, is the noble truth of the cessation of sorrow: it is the cessation of all trace of desire ... perfect detachment. This, O monks, is the noble truth of the way: it is the way that leads to the cessation of sorrow, the

holy way with eight branches: rightness of opinion, rightness of intention, rightness of word, rightness of bodily
activity, rightness of the means of existence, rightness of
effort, rightness of attention, rightness of mental concentration. (*Samyutta nikaya* 5,240)

Each of these right attitudes was used in a variety of ways
including physical exercises and meditation, which the
monk had to practise for long periods each day. All this
called for severe discipline and conditions of life impractica-
ble for those who had family or professional obligations.
The complete initiate of Buddhism, therefore, like the
Blessed One himself, had to leave his family in order to lead
the life of a mendicant monk and submit himself to the rules
established by the Buddha for his first disciples.

The most elementary principle of conduct was confidence
in the refuge of the 'Three Jewels', following the sacred
formulae:-

> I take refuge in the Buddha,
> I take refuge in the Dharma,
> I take refuge in the Sangha.

The *Buddha* is considered as a sure guide, the *Dharma* as
his liberating teaching, and the *Sangha* as the milieu which
provides favourable conditions for working out his teaching. There followed the ten rules for good conduct:-

To abstain from killing any living thing and from taking
what is not given, to resist every temptation against
chastity, to keep from lying, from fermented drink, from
eating after midday, from dancing, singing, playing music
or attending worldly festivals, from carrying garlands
and from the use of perfumes or cosmetics, from using
large or raised beds, from accepting money.

(*Khuddhaka – Patha*)

Other versions of the ten rules, developing the idea of lying,
classify what is evil in three categories according as it has its
origin in the body, the word or the thought.

Thus, rejecting the extreme asceticism of the *sannyâsis* of the Jain type, as well as the sacrifices of the Brahmins, the Buddha chose a 'middle path' with non-violence, chastity and poverty as fundamental virtues opposed to the capital sins of passion, hatred and self-deception.

The *bhikshu*, then, must spare the life of the smallest insect and practise chastity of body and mind. Any serious failure in these virtues condemned the monk to expulsion. Respect for life was closely bound up with belief in reincarnation, and the repression of the sexual instinct was normal in a religion aiming at the elimination of desire. Poverty consisted in possessing nothing of one's own beyond the habit one wore, toilet necessities and the begging bowl, mendicancy being, in the context of the time, the most natural expression of renunciation of property.

Detailed directives further limited begging to what was strictly necessary. Clothes were received at fixed times and all solid food was forbidden after noon. The duty of begging for one's food each day and of eating without discrimination whatever was given, was regarded as an exercise of non-desire and, by the effort of mastery over the senses and thoughts that it implied, as favourable to the development of virtues.[4]

Watchfulness over the senses and particularly over the eyes was continued on the return from begging and during the whole day:

Let the eye not wander about like the bee of the forests, like the timid deer of the woods or the frightened child. The eyes should be lowered and look at nothing beyond the length of a yoke; let the monk not be the slave of the power of thoughts like the restless bee.

(*Digha Nigaya*, II, 293)

The effects of this moral discipline were reinforced by prolonged meditation on the repugnant aspects of the body, used as an antidote to the appetite for pleasure. The analytical spirit of Buddhism delighted also in dividing sensation into various components: the exterior stimulus, the perception by the senses, the reaction of these and the arousing of desire. This objective reflection made a passionate response impossible and controlled the admission of thoughts into the mind or the mind's acceptance of them:

> As rain cannot penetrate a well-thatched house, so desire cannot penetrate a well-trained mind.
>
> (Dharmapada, Twin verses, 14)

Similar methods were used to neutralize different perceptions and emotions so as to arrive at that state of perfect calm which enabled one to pass beyond the impermanence of this world to the attainment of Nirvana, the absolute tranquillity of the Ocean of Peace.

To fight against the evils issuing from the word, there are forty methods of concentration (samadhi) to use according to the needs and temperament of each person. They take as their starting point a physical image, for example, a circle of pale red sand, or of blue flowers, a bowl of water, an image of the Buddha or of someone loved and respected. In regarding this object attentively, one gains a very vivid mental picture which remains when the eyes are closed. The attention is sustained by the repetition of words appropriate to the object contemplated, for example, 'sand, sand', or 'flowers, flowers ...'. The concentration progresses step by step and gradually one masters the eight dhyanas or degrees of meditation: by attention to the mental object the mind is liberated from the world of the senses. Next, one passes beyond this discursive thought by 'faith', an attitude of confidence and desire for something above the material; from this comes a feeling of peace. One must advance above this sensation of well-being towards a state of purity of spirit and serenity of mood that one strives to make all-embracing. The spirit then becomes 'empty' with neither perception nor non-perception and seems to establish an almost physical contact with Nirvana, losing touch with the material world in a kind of transitory ecstasy.[5]

Another form of meditation is practised to free oneself from the evil arising out of thoughts. It consists in being attentive to every movement of the body, to any sensations, desires or thoughts that may chance to come. One begins by mentally concentrating on a part of the body, the tip of the nose or the distension of the stomach produced by respiration. Each movement, sensation and even distraction must be recognized and its name pronounced. Every necessary movement must be made slowly and consciously, repeating its name. This concentration proceeds through thirteen stages of mental experiences, one of which is the perception of the body as composed of a cluster of elements which disintegrate, and of the soul as a mass of sparks. Thus the monk is led to complete detachment from matter and from the mind and finally comes to rest in *Nirvana*.

Concentration on the 'four illimited' applies the same principle to the emotions. Its aim is to break the barriers between the self and others. The first step is to develop a universal benevolence:

Let everyone be happy and at ease; let him be joyous and secure ... Let no-one deceive or despise another, whoever he may be. Let no-one in anger or ill-will desire evil for another. As a mother guards and protects her only son, so does one love without limit all living beings, spreading goodwill over the whole world. (*Metta Sutta*)

After goodwill comes compassion, then sympathy in joy and in a synthesis of all emotions one finds perfect tranquillity and repose in the peace beyond all feeling. Another series of exercises concerns the reactions of man to the occult powers. Primitive Buddhism professed a certain scorn for these. Later other schools, particularly those of tantrism, were to value them highly.

Pursuing their analysis, Buddhist monks were to discover at the centre of desire, the 'self', which is the link between perceptions and emotions, and the plane of the mental and reasoning faculties. 'Wisdom' or methodical meditation on the teaching of the *Dharma*, aims at demonstrating the emptiness of this 'self'. This is the object of the *Abhidharma* a study which analyses reality and reduces it to five *skandhas* or components: material forms, feeling, perception, consciousness, the reciprocal action of impersonal powers. Thus the self, as the source of desire for possessions, is eliminated; it is reduced to an identity with the ultimate reality, beyond deception by the senses, beyond ignorance and desire, the state of *Nirvana*, in this case also called the *Dharma*. The treatise of the *Dharmapada* sums all this up in two concise sentences:

> All weighty matters cause distress; when through wisdom one has discovered this, one is disgusted with evil; this is the truth.
> All things are without souls; when through wisdom one has discovered this, one is disgusted with evil; this is the truth. (*Magga Vagga* 278–279)

The monk who, with courage and perseverance, has travelled the whole way, has succeeded in drying up the source of desire. He has reached a state of perfect detachment, in contact, even in this life, with infinite peace; he is the *Arhat*, the saint:

> For him who has finished the journey, whose spirit is undisturbed, who is freed from all things and has destroyed all bonds; for him the fever of passion no longer exists ... Oh, how happy are the Arhats! In them is no more passionate desire; pride in the self is uprooted and broken is the snare of illusion. Set free from the passions, their spirits are resplendent... With perfect mastery over themselves, these men have conquered the world.
> (*Arahanta Vagga*, 90; *Samyatta Nikaya*, 3, 83–84)

The ideal of this solitary pursuit of perfection 'after the manner of a rhinoceros', is not lacking in grandeur. It is perhaps reminiscent of that of the Hindu sannyasi, but differs from it in an essential way. The Hindu monk, in most cases, is committed with all his being to the pursuit of union with the Absolute: He is one of those who:

> Through austerity, chastity, faith and knowledge, seek for the Self ... the eternal, the fearless, the final goal, from whence there is no return.
> (*Prashna Upanishad*, 1, 10)

This progress in the search for union with the eternal was of its nature without return. In Hinduism, giving up the monastic life was generally considered a defeat, a serious fault. As for the Buddhist, he aimed at improving the condition of his soul or his attitude to material things. He might one day decide that he had reached the goal he sought or, on the other hand, that it was beyond his attainment in this life and must be postponed till a later reincarnation. A monk's life was thus considered by many of those who embarked upon it to be something like a school, where a man makes a certain amount of progress and then leaves; only a very small number persevering to the attainment of higher wisdom. The return to the world thus became normal; in Thailand it is even consecrated in a special ceremony.

The different Schools of Buddhist Monachism

The austerity of the monastic way of salvation had another consequence. Gradually the importance attached to compassion in the primitive teaching was developed and gave rise to new schools which, in broadening the way of salvation, set themselves against the 'way of the Ancients' or *Theravada*, known also as *Hinayana* or 'small Vehicle'. These new tendencies were to modify the monastic ideal considerably as well as the relations between monks and lay people.

The *bhikshus* had always realized the duty of preaching to the laity encouraging them towards good. Of this, the impressive number of missionary monks who, throughout the ages, have journeyed to spread Buddhism to other lands, bears eloquent witness. Compassion, as we have seen, was always one of the monk's cardinal virtues, but changing circumstances were to accelerate the development of these tendencies.

The third king of the dynasty of Mauryas, the great Ashoka, had been inspired by Buddhism to establish a kind of state religion; the Sounga dynasty, which followed at the beginning of the second century B.C., was opposed to this. Deprived of state subsidies, the *bhikshus* found themselves

solely dependent on the faithful laity and were thus led to
devote more zealous effort towards their spiritual progress.
A few chosen monks, pitying the multitudes, took their
interests to heart and tried to find an easier way of salvation
for them than the rigorous monastic life. At the same period
also the *Bhakti* movement in India which sought salvation
in the 'devotion' or loving confidence in a god, was gaining
its full strength. Moving in the same direction, the
Buddhists were to develop the way of 'faith', a saving confidence in the Buddha, maintained by the repeated invocation
of his name. At the same time, the primitive historical character of Buddha was assuming the nature of a super-worldly
being, of whom Gautama was only one of many incarna-
tions. Each of these new Buddhas had the right to a special
devotion under the ministry of the monks. The devotee,
after his death, was believed to be reborn in the Paradise of
this Buddha, who then completed his instruction and
allowed him finally to attain *Nirvana*.[6]

A new development of the doctrine of compassion found
yet other means of gaining salvation. In fact, viewed from
the angle of detachment and compassion, the ideal of the
Arhat, concentrated as it was on the acquisition of merits to
attain Nirvana, seemed egotistical. The perfect man, on the
contrary, must:

> make a gift of his merits and consecrate them to the
> enlightenment of others.
>
> > (*Santideva, Bodhicaryavatara*, III, 6)

These generous souls were the *Bodhisattvas*, who after
attaining perfection, postponed till later their approach to
Nirvana so as to help others to reach it and, to bring this
about, they made a vow to transfer to others all their
merits.[7] The fertile imagination of the monks multiplied
new saviours and proposed them as models for the devotion
of the faithful. The ideal pursued was thus no longer that of
the *Arhat*, but the *Bodhisattva*, accomplishing universal
salvation in the course of innumerable mortal lives. In his
monastic profession, the novice was to proclaim:

May I, in a world without refuge, without shelter, without safety, without island, be the help, the refuge, the shelter, the safety, the island. May I cross, for all who have not crossed it, the ocean of existences; may I lead into Nirvana those who are not already there and console those who are desolate. (*Bodhisattva Pratimoksa Sutra*)

The development of speculation on the nature of Buddha, the devotion to the *Bodhisattvas* and the notion of the transference of merits led to an expansion of the old way of suppressing grief into a religion of a salvation, such as characterises the Buddhism of *Mahayana*, 'the great vehicle' or more exactly, 'the great course'.[8]

Although the framework of the old rules remained intact and though sometimes monks of different schools even lived in the same *avasa*, this new ideal modified monastic life quite profoundly. Certainly the eremitical state, in which one moved in silence towards perfection, continued to exist, but most other monks, prompted by compassion, made their chief concern the spiritual advancement and the material well-being of the faithful. The *bhikshus* thus became ministers for the devotion of the laity and the promoters of works of charity.

Profiting from the only work permitted to them by the Buddha, that of maintaining and improving their buildings, the monks became experts in this field themselves or encouraged guilds of artists and outstanding architects. In every place where they settled, from India to Japan or Vietnam, passing through Kashmir, central Asia and China, or to the south, through Ceylon, Burma, Thailand, Laos, Cambodia, Malaysia, and as far as Java, they created large groups of buildings whose works of art still arouse our admiration.

Their efforts throughout many centuries to translate Buddhist teachings into other languages, gave rise to important intellectual and literary developments in the culture of the countries of Asia.[9] The monks opened hospitals and schools which, in certain regions, have been the only ones existing in the country for several centuries. Having now become ministers of worship, the *bhikshus* often left their isolated cells to live near a temple. To promote devotions and pilgrimages, they were led to found hostelries for travellers and to build roads and bridges. They, too, were responsible for the introduction into the Far East of financial customs practised in India, such as giving loans on pledge, auction sales and lotteries. Another activity which flourished particularly in China, combined finance with devotion; this was the custom of declaring the monastery 'a fertile field', where any alms deposited yielded innumerable merits.

Having become rich and influential the monks meddled with politics and in Tibet even went so far as to take into their hands the whole administration of the country. But elsewhere too, riches and power were almost always a source of decadence and often gave rise to persecution.

In adapting themselves to the different cultures of the countries where they settled, the Buddhists succumbed to their influence. The mixture of different religious currents gave rise to numerous groups, and certain among them had their own distinctive form of monachism.

New Aspects of Buddhism in China, Japan and Tibet

Buddhism in China

Buddhism, in its different schools, began to be brought into China in the 1st century and was flourishing in the country by the 4th. Under the influence of Taoism, it joined together the Buddha and Tao as the cosmic law of nature and the impersonal Absolute.

According to the tradition, around the year 520, Bodhidharma, an Indian master of meditation, arrived in China where he made a number of disciples. His doctrine united the teachings of the *Mahayana* and Tao. His insistence upon meditation (*Ch'an* in Chinese – the transcription of the Sanskrit *dhyana* which became Zen in Japanese) led to his being regarded as the originator of Zen.

In the 8th century the disciples of Bodhidharma formed two distinct branches, in the north and south of China. The northern branch taught that there was a progressive enlightenment: it insisted on the preparatory exercises and the struggle against the passions which would 'dust the mirror' of the soul. This branch gradually died out.

The founder of the southern school, Hui Neng (683–713) is said to have been an illiterate child who had learnt Zen by experience. For him and his group the passions were as illusory as the self: there was neither dust nor mirror. Enlightenment would happen suddenly, bringing about a union of the spirit with the Buddha-Nature, guaranteeing the non-operation of the passions, the disappearance of the self and the cessation of mental activity.

Buddhism flourished greatly in the 8th century, but in 845 there was a persecution which spared only Amidism and the two Zen schools of the south: the *Rinzai*, which used Koans gathered together into collections, and the *Soto*, which used predominantly meditation. Under the Song dynasty (960–1261) these two schools had a great influence on the development of art and philosophy in China. They passed to Japan at the beginning of the 12th century.

In these various different schools, the personal discipline required by meditation meant that the new disciple needed to be carefully guided by a master, and so the disciple-master relationship sprang up as a basis for monastic life: a famous master would set himself up in some area and the 'postulants' would assemble round him to follow his teaching. When he grew old, he would pass on the teaching to the best of his disciples and instruct him to teach the others. The large number of monks living in the monasteries made it necessary to modify the traditional rules, imported from India. The cold climate and the great number of persons to be fed in remote places meant that begging was not sufficient for their needs. Manual labour, tolerated by the Buddha as a means of stabilizing the minds of his less cultivated monks, thus became a necessity while continuing to be a means of meditation.

It seem that it was the master Pai-Chan (749–764) who gave the note of originality to these rules, keeping the firm discipline of ancient Buddhism but introducing the obligation of manual labour. 'A day without work is a day without food' was one of his favourite sayings – and until his old age he showed by example the way to do it. In the monastic day, work alternated with worship and meditation. Other regulations laid down the disposition of the buildings, the hierarchy of the officials, the variations in the ascetic practices for each season and the penances imposed for infringements of the rules.

At the same time, the other branches of Buddhism continued to develop – especially Amidism.

Buddhism in Japan

Buddhism was introduced into Japan around the 6th century and several of its schools were already in existence in the 13th century: some of recent origin (*Amidism* and *Nishiren*), others (especially *Tendai* and *Shingon*) were old and powerful. All of them continued alongside the two schools of Zen introduced at this period: *Rinzai* and *Soto*.

Rinzai, introduced by Eisai (1141–1215) increased in size rapidly and at the time of Kamakura (12th c.) had a great impact on Japanese art (temple architecture, painting, calligraphy, ceramics, pottery and lacquer work). The school continued the *Koan* method and the monastic traditions emanating from China.

The school of *Soto* was founded in Japan by Master Dogen (1200–1253), a man of deep meditation. During a long visit to China, he discovered a master who had learnt from the great tradition. When he returned to Japan, disciples gathered round him and he taught Zazen, meditation in a seated position.

Many other schools were founded after this and some of them fell away from Buddhist orthodoxy by adopting a moral indifference which led to many abuses and allowed for the institution of monk-soldiers. In the troubled periods at the end of the 10th and 16th centuries, armies were levied to defend the monks' goods against the incursions of a feudal and centralising state. In modern times some new schools have started, extracting various elements of the preceding traditions to make new syntheses, suitable to the needs of the times. But it is the Zen schools which have had the most influence outside Japan.[10]

Zen

Bodhidharma, who came across Tao in China, was led to emphasise an aspect of *Mahayana* Buddhism, which regards the presence of the infinite in the heart of each being as the only true reality. This presence, discovered by the Buddha during his enlightenment, is called the 'Buddha-nature' or 'Buddheity'. The way out of the cycle of rebirth is found by immersion in and fusion with this Absolute Reality, this Ocean of Peace, which is present in all beings and does not admit of any kind of qualification. The individual self disappears by pouring itself out in this blessed communion with the Universe at its source.

This fusion in the Absolute supposes a separation from the finite world, whether it be from the material domain, the world of the senses or the realm of intellectual concepts. The subject passes beyond all of this to find a profound silence in which the 'Buddha-nature' can shine.

The final union is prepared for, and can even be experienced here below, by this effort of separation and by a concentration which brings about an interior silence. This deep silence makes it possible for the disciple to be connected with his inner self, the 'heart of the Buddha' present in all beings. Enlightenment is this tentative communion with the Universe in the Absolute which lives in it – an experience which is salvific and which is sought after with all possible energy.

The ways (or *dô*, in Japanese) of obtaining this experience are as diverse as the methods and the various activities involved in the search. There is the way of flowers (*Kadô*), the way of archery (*Kyudô*), the tea ceremony (*Sadô*), painting, calligraphy (*Shodô*) and, above all, Zendo (*Zazendô*), the meditation in a seated posture of Zazen.

Seated in the lotus position, the back straight, breathing controlled, the monk begins by chanting some sutras, an act which gains merit, sustains the posture of the body, keeps the breathing rhythmic, and pervades his entire being with spiritual energy. After that, silence and attentiveness to the present moment remove the superficial agitation of the spirit, just as muddy water, which is allowed to stay still in a glass, becomes clear when the mud sinks to the bottom.

So, having left behind thought and feelings, the spirit becomes clear and empty so as to welcome the ever-present Infinite and loses itself in it.

This profound awareness of the Infinite at the base of one's being – an awareness which comes about either by gradual revelation or in a flash of intuition is called enlightenment, the awakening or *samadhi*. The experience of being in relation with the Essential, places the concern of the one who meditates above the agitation of the senses and desires. It allows him to 'return to the market place', that is to the ordinary life of society, with a clear and calm spirit, knowing how to view things in their true light.

Tibetan Buddhism

Coming from India, Buddhism penetrated Tibet and enjoyed royal protection in the 7th century. It was a form of *Mahayana* using the tantric practices, like the *Bön-po* religion of the country – and this facilitated its diffusion. The Indian master Padmasambhava (otherwise known as the Guru Rimpoche) is venerated as the founder of Tibetan Buddhism and of its most ancient school, *Nyingmapa*.

From the 8th century an enormous work of translation of the sanskrit texts was undertaken. The precision of the vocabulary that was used, or created, makes them one of the best sources for understanding ancient Buddhism, whose original sanskrit texts have disappeared.

In the 9th century a persecution and the fall of the reigning dynasty (842) almost wiped out Buddhism from the country. But one hundred years later the school of *Nyingmapa*, which had survived, reconstituted itself into a monastic order, which venerated Padmasambhava as equal of the Buddha. The *Sakyapa* order originated in a branch of the *Nyingmapa*, to become an independent movement, for a time, that ruled all Tibet (1270–1340).

The arrival of other Indian masters led to the creation of new schools: Atisa, builder of the temple of Re ting, is the originator of the school of *Kadampa*. In the same way the school of *Kagyupa* was established by Naropa. His disciple Marpa came to Tibet and was a great translator. He was the master of the lay mystic Milarepa. A little later Gampopa introduced the monastic discipline into the movement and is the originator of several branches of the *Kagyupa*.

Around 1200 the work of translation which had been going on for four centuries reached its conclusion and so the canon of Tibetan scriptures was formed, divided into two parts: the *Kanjur*, 100 volumes of teachings attributed to the Buddha, and containing the Sutras (wisdom texts to be chanted), the *Tantra* (formulas and rituals) and the *Vinaya* (monastic discipline); the *Tanjur* has 250 volumes of treatises, commentaries and hymns.

In the 14th century, Tsong ka pa, who had been given his formation at Re Ting, the monastery of Atisa, founded the great monastery of Ganden and the order of **Gelugpa** which reformed monastic life with strict rules. This new fervour led to the creation of other great monasteries, like Sera and Drepung. The support of the Mongols gave the Dalai Lama, the head of the order, a great political influence and the 5th Dalai Lama became Head of the State of Lhasa in the mid 17th century.

This reform had a positive effect on the other Orders, giving rise to a renewal of discipline and study. The *Gelugpa* school, whose followers wore the *Yellow Cap*, distinguishing itself in the study of philosophy and logic, while the others, called the *Red Caps* focused on meditation and tantric rituals. Tibet was originally divided into several kingdoms and each order was dominant in a particular region, a fact which led to a struggle for supremacy among them, whose effects can still be felt.

The 19th century was a period of stagnation in which the country became isolated and wanted to close its borders to strangers. Independence came to an end in 1950 with the invasion by China. The monasteries were destroyed, the Dalai Lama and a part of the population took refuge in India where they strove to preserve and disseminate throughout the world their culture and their monastic life, while building monasteries in exile which revived the names and traditions of those in Tibet.

Besides those who are rightly called monks and who live in monasteries or hermitages and wear a sombre dark red habit, there are also some tantric ascetics (*Ngag pa*) whose

long hair flows over their white habit with a red band. They
do not live in community and are answerable solely to their
guru. Last there are the Yogis (*Tag den*) whose master-disci-
ple relationship is even stronger.

But this relationship does not confine itself simply to the
transmission of doctrine but goes on to find the reincarnation of the dead master in a child (*tulku*) who is discovered
by means of a series of tests. There are a great many such
tests for the Abbots of the large monasteries and, above all,
for the Dalai Lama. The Panchen Lama, official guardian of
doctrine was also chosen in a similar way.

The Tibetan way, the Vajrayana

Vajrayana means 'diamond vehicle': Vajra is lightning
considered as a supernatural substance, as hard as diamond
and as transparent as space; it is thus identified as the
Ultimate Reality. The follower, using study, meditation and
the rituals finds once more his 'true nature' of 'diamond
body', and is identified with the Ultimate.

Education and studies

The monasteries are schools and the largest are considered
as universities. The monks in them learn a fixed number of
texts which constitute their diverse levels of study. The title
of *Geshe* is given in the *Gelugpa* school, to those who attain
the highest degree. A *Lama* is a master of doctrine who has
made, at least once, the great retreat, lasting three years.
The Tibetan monks emphasize the community as an important factor of formation and also the virtue of kindness
which creates a happy atmosphere for the young recruits.

Meditation

Meditation is the most important part of monastic life. The
retreats of the *Nyingmapa* and *Kagyupa* are periods of
seclusion which last 3 years, 3 months and 3 days. This
exercise of meditation is considered to be a means of
bypassing conceptual thought so as to experience the ultimate nature of the spirit, the state of Buddha in
non-dualism. This happens in three steps: reception of the
teaching; reflection, which explores the meaning of the

teaching; and meditation, properly so-called. From here one moves towards an intuitive realisation by developing kindness, which destroys egoism, and wisdom which sets free from dualism.

The two principal forms of meditation are:

Shine, which looks towards inner pacification by silencing discursive thought. As a start, one takes a material or mental object as a 'prop', such as a bowl of water, or an aspect of the Buddha or of a deity, viewed in peace and serenity. The body becomes like a stranger and the spirit calm and pure, in a state of happiness.

Laktong: based on the deep calm of Shine, one undertakes the analysis of phenomena and of the self, so as to understand that, at base they have no reality. Then, moving beyond conceptual analysis, the spirit returns to itself in the present moment, relaxed, beyond fear and anxiety. These intense and brief moments, beyond thought or in the gap between two thoughts, must be repeated frequently. The merits thus gained are applied to other people.

Tantra
Tantra uses devotion (*bhakti*) to a divinity of one's choice (*yidam*) which becomes a personification of spiritual and magic forces. For each divinity there are special initiations, general instructions, specific practice instructions, all governed by a vow to practise (in or out of retreat) until realisation is obtained. This realisation enables one to know and become intimate with the deity, and finally to identify oneself with it and share in its powers. These instructions and practice governed by the vow are handed down through the succession of masters and are necessary to perform some religious or superhuman acts or to attain some mystical states.[11]

Tibetan tantrism considers itself to be a short road to the attainment of superior states of being and of non-duality. It is characterised by its method of spiritual ascesis, based not on the rejection of obstacles but on their transformation. It teaches that all reality can be favourable or contrary depending on the state of consciousness of the disciple. This double aspect is shown in the hundreds of deities venerated – sometimes good, sometimes terrible, helping or protecting the devotee. In the same way the emotions provoked by the passions are brought into use in order to master rather than reject them and deliberate use is made of the body as an aid to the spirit.

There is a similar complementarity between passive discernment and action or between wisdom and compassion: the first is considered as feminine, and the other masculine. They are attributed to gods and goddesses for whom sexual union is the symbol used to rise above dualism. However ancient practices of actual sexual union as a yogic process are known and taught in a restricted way.

The main Tantric practices are: the repetition of certain *mantras*, the *mandala*, as a representation of the divinity, with its spiritual and cosmic connotations; the *ritual gestures* which have also a magic effectiveness, and finally *dances* in which passions and virtues are represented by animals, portrayed by masks and costumes. Dances and *mandalas* are forms of meditation involving the body. In the temples, the most venerated images are the spiritual masters, the head of the lineage, and the divinities such as *Avalokiteshvara* the compassionate, whose multiple arms symbolise his attributes. There is also the goddess *Tara* whose various aspects are represented by different colours (white, green ...)

As a whole the ways of meditation of the Buddhist schools seem to aim at dissipating what most of them believe to be a fundamental error, that is conceptualizing separate identities. At a deeper level, one discovers that, beyond all reality, when the self has disappeared, there remains *Shunyata* (emptiness), the ultimate Infinite nature of all reality, Absolute and eternal. This seems to be a contradiction with the Christian faith which believes in God as a Creator, loving human beings. Nevertheless, there are profound convergences between the two religions: both consider mastery of the passions and refusal of any egoism as a necessary condition to reach the Absolute. The final aim of all is union with the Infinite, present in the depths of every human being, and unique source of the Universe.

Notes

1 For most of the quotations from Buddhist texts, we have used the following works: E. Conze, *Buddhism; Dhammapada*, translation by Nerada Thera, Colombo; 'Dhammapada', translation by Ven. Narada Maha Thera in *The path of Buddhism,* Colombo; *The Great Asian Religions, an Anthology,* by Wing-tsit Cham; *Ordination Procedure,* Mahamakutarajavidyalaya, Bangkok; *Some Sayings of the Buddha,* translated by F.L. Woodward; Dr. Panabokke, *Unpublished Thesis,* University of Ceylon, Colombo. This last work, as well as the book of Sukumar Dutt, *The Buddha and Two Centuries After,* supply much information on the beginnings of Buddhism; on meditation, see also L. Nu. *Buddhism,* in the *Bhavan Journal, 2/75.*

2 In the main, it is to these solitary or wandering monks that we owe the spread of Buddhism beyond India and the periodic renewals of fervour in the Far East which has kept it alive till our own times.

3 It seems, however, that in the Zen monasteries of Japan, the Abbot is generally the Spiritual Master of the monks.

4 With the acceptance by the monks of invitations to eat with lay people and of gifts in money and kind, mendicancy, as a practice of asceticism, has disappeared in many countries. It remains as an exercise for the novice in Japanese Zen. On the subject of celibacy it is interesting to note that in Buddhism as also in Hinduism, it was practised as long as the monk consecrated himself to the search for the world beyond, either on his own behalf or for the faithful over whom he eventually had charge. It disappeared when his function shrank to that of the celebration of a cult or was infected with the practice of magic. The historical evolution of different groups and their usages provide evidence for this.

5 The mahayanist school, pursuing this analysis, were to insist on 'the extinction of the self', but at the same time were to present *Nirvana* as a 'state of omniscience'.

6 One of the most famous was the Buddha Amida, worshipped especially in China and Japan.

7 The idea of the giving and transference of merits is now familiar also to many of the Theravadins, as the hymn that ends the evening prayer of the monks of Thailand bears witness:

> May the merits acquired by me, now or at other times, be shared among all beings, in number infinite, immeasurable; those who are dear and virtuous as Father and Mother, beings visible and invisible, indifferent or hostile ... May they all, and for all time, have a life happy and free from hatred, may they find the sure way and may all their desires be granted. (Ordination Procedure p. 72.)

8 The Buddhism of *Theravada* or 'Small Vehicle' is predominant in Sri Lanka, Burma, Thailand, Laos and Cambodia; but it has adopted many of the ways of the 'Great Vehicle'. In other countries the *Mahayana* ('Great Vehicle') is predominant.

9　The short mimed sketches, alternating with recited prayers and chants, used by the Buddhist missionaries, influenced the Chinese theatre. The use of the vernacular tongue in the sermons and the problems posed by translating their terms into Chinese led to developments in language and phonetics. The various branches of art – painting, sculpture, architecture, music – experienced a similar revival in the greater part of the country subjected to Buddhist influence. For example, the monks introduced the use of stone, the storeyed tower, frescoes and the great rupestral santuaries. The school of painting in the monastery of Sung in China marked an epoch and influenced Japanese Zen painting. Other schools specialised in flute playing, Japanese literature (12th to 13th centuries) and Buddhist writings. (cf. *Encyclopedia Universalis*. art. cit.; and H. Dumoulin, *A History of Zen Buddhism*). It must be noted, however, that in spite of considerable intellectual effort, Buddhism took several centuries to integrate with Chinese and Japanese cultures. Introduced into China at the beginning of the Christian era, it did not expand in any real sense until the fifth century. Similarly in Japan it came in successive waves from the sixth century onwards, but was not fully integrated till the thirteenth. During the early centuries, it appeared as an alien religion, practised chiefly among intellectual circles.

10　Most of our information on the development of Zen comes from H. Dumoulin *A History of Zen Buddhism*.

11　These initiations, or passing of energy, aim at putting oneself under the protection of a god or entering into communion with other beings (the *guru* or other forces) possessing a force that the novice can obtain thanks to the psychic waves in which he is immersed during the ceremony. This often included the absorption of water and actions by the *guru*, accompanied by recited prayers (*mantras*) but higher initiations, it seems, were made by silent psychic communication between the *guru* and the disciple, who remain sitting face to face for several hours. cf. A David Neel, *Initiations and initiates in Tibet, passim.*

CHAPTER 3

Monasticism and Egyptian Religions

There is no monachism as such in the old Egyptian religions. Nevertheless some aspects of their religious traditions are of the highest interest to the monastic historian. Amid the jungle of popular polytheism, they demonstrate that in theological circles the finest thinkers were familiar with themes that are basic to monasticism: the uniqueness of God; His providence and love for man; man's self-surrender to Him through love; and the human craving for solitude and silence in order to promote the search for Him in the depth of the heart.

The belief in God's uniqueness is found in texts[1] dating back to the old Empire, to the middle of the third millennium B.C. These portray the great gods as various aspects of the one god, unique and unnamed, the secondary deities being but His emanations, and all created by Him. Recently discovered hymns summarize this ancient tradition:

Amon, Re, Ptah, all three are gods, none is like to them;
Amon is His name as hidden,
Re is His face, and
Ptah His body

(*Papyrus of Leyde*, 350, IV, 21–22)

Unique form creating all that is,
One who is unique, creating all beings,
Men came out of His two eyes
And the gods came into being on His lips.

(Hymn to Amon of Cairo, VI, 2–5;
in *Amour de la Vie*, p. 97)

This supreme God is not far away from men; Providence, powerful and benevolent, it is

> He who hears the petitions of the sorrowful,
> Whose heart is kind for those who beseech Him,
> Who frees the meek from the hand of the violent,
> Who decides between the poor and the mighty.
> (Pap. 17 of Boulaq IV, 4–5; in *Amour de la Vie*, p. 99)

God is also man's shepherd, and He expects from His faithful that sincerity of heart which is more acceptable than wealthy offerings – namely, honesty and justice.

> Men's hearts can rely on this:
> The virtue of an upright heart is pleasing to God,
> To be preferred to the bull of the unjust.
> Work for God and He will work for you...
> God knows well those who do Him service,
> The men of God's flock are well provided-for:
> For them He has made heaven and earth,
> For their sake He repelled the monster of the deep;
> He has created the spirit so that their nostrils breathe,
> For they are images of Him, issuing from Himself.
> (Teaching of King Aktoes – third dynasty –
> to his son, Merikara, 2100–2080 B.C.;
> in *Amour de la Vie*, pp. 102–3)

> He saves whom He loves, even though he be fallen into hades,
> He frees from fate as He chooses,
> He has eyes and ears.
> For those whom He loves, how far soever He may be.
> He hears the supplications of all who call upon Him.
> He comes from afar with instant reply to the one who cries out to Him ...
> King God with thoughts of loving kindness
> To Him belongs the man eager to hear His call;
> He is of more help than thousands to those who have enshrined Him in their hearts.
> (Hymn to Amon. ch. 70, in *Amour de la Vie*, p. 122)

Man responds to this God who is both Creator and
Provider, with praise and love. It was customary to wear
amulets on which were engraved short poems such as:

> Whosoever loves justice is hallowed by Re
> My happiness is to behold Amon,
> Amon-Re is the refuge of the afflicted,
> To love Amon-Re is the protection of my life.
> The servant of Amon is the man who does His will.
> God's holy one will live for ever.
>
> (Written on a scarab; *Hermès* No. 4, p. 24)

A deeper love still, finds expression in certain other hymns.
In the following, after a salutation to Amon as Sun-God, the
poet continues with many comparisons, and ends with the
avowal of man's inability to represent God under a material
form; love alone is a fit response to His love:

> Hail to you who dwell in the peace of your temple,
> Lord of joy and dazzling manifestations...
> Your beauty delights the heart
> Your love overpowers
> Your perfect form makes hands fall limp,
> The heart that beholds you forgets all else.
>
> (Pap. Boulaq, 17, V, 4–VI, 2;
> in *Amour de la Vie*, p. 121)

The natural consequence of love is to follow God's will
with fidelity:

> He who obeys God will follow the right path,
> Happy the man whose heart inclines him toward it,
> Whose heart is steadfast in God's way.
> His life here below is strengthened,
> He whose soul is filled with the fear of God
> Will find great happiness on earth.
>
> (Inscription on Petosiris' tomb;
> in *Amour de la Vie*, p. 136)

But devotees trust to God's grace to become perfect, a condition summed up in the phrase 'having a true voice.'

> May Thou be my support each morning.
> Come, O Divine Word, when I enter the presence of the
> Lord God
> So that I may go forth having a true voice.
>   (Pap. Salier, I, VIII, 2–6; in *Amour de la Vie*, p. 131)

Scrutinizing the various aspects of our relations with God, the Great, the Unique, Egyptians discovered also the mystery of the hidden God,

> No God came before Him...
> The Almighty whose birth is mysterious,
> Who has created His own beauty,
> The divine God who brought Himself into existence...
> No God knows his true form,
> His image is not portrayed in books,
> No perfect witness to him can be given,
> He is too mysterious for his glory to be revealed,
> He is too great to be scrutinized, too powerful to be
> known,
> Fear might strike a man dead on the spot,
> If his sacred name that nobody can know was spoken
> out.
> Not even a God can invoke him by name
> Hidden-Soul he is called, so ineffable is He.
>   (Pap. Leyde, ch. 40; ch. 200; *Amour de la Vie*, p. 118).

In the face of God's greatness, the most eloquent words are powerless, and the only attitude towards his mystery is silence:

> Do not interrogate God; God will not tolerate violence and his form cannot be apprehended by human sight. Be careful not to raise your voice in his house; God likes silence.
>   (Pap. Chester Beauty, IV, 5, 1–12;
>   *Amour de la Vie*, p. 126)

Another moralist, the scribe Anii (18th dynasty, 16th–14th cent. B.C.) gives a piece of advice which is a real invitation to deep silent prayer of the heart:

Do not multiply words,
Keep silent if you want to be happy,
Do not raise your voice in the peaceful house of God,
He hates shouting.
When you pray with a loving heart,
The words of which are hidden,
He gives you what you need,
He hears what you say,
He accepts your offering.
(Pap. Cairo IV, 1–2; in *Hermès* No. 4, p. 17)

A little later the wise Amenope – well-known now that his writings have been connected with the Book of Proverbs – adopts an image characteristic of the Old Testament, to describe two kinds of men. The man of fiery temper is like a jungle tree whose branches are cut down for general use, and fire is its final shroud. On the other hand:

The true silent man dwells apart,
He is like a tree growing in an orchard.
Evergreen, it yields a double crop,
It abides in the temple of the Lord;
Sweet its fruit and pleasant its shade,
Its final end will be the Garden.
(Amenope. Teaching; ch. 4; *Amour de la Vie*, p. 125)

Why did this aptitude for silence not develop in monastic life? Possibly because in such a society individuals were too closely knit to the group; or perhaps because this mystical current was far from being the mainstream of Egyptian religious thought – it resembled rather a small plant which can reach its full flowering only when Christianity has cleared away the forest of polytheism stifling its growth.

All the same this silent search into the mystery of God found outward expression in Egypt in at least two instances. In the first place, some pilgrims used to go and spend a few days in the desert caves near Thebes 'to see Amon' or the goddess Meret Seger 'who likes silence'. The graffiti written on the walls leave no doubt as to the intentions of visitors:

> Praise be to Amon
> Who remains the Unique
> And takes on the form of thousands...
> Amon, give me your heart,
> Bow down your ear to me,
> Open your eyes,
> Save me every day.
> (*Hermès* No. 4, p. 24)

Secondly there was a curious band of devotees who lived in the temple enclosure of the God Serapis in Memphis, 'Kept within the walls by God's power which summoned them', they devoted themselves to a life of silence, poverty and worship, at least for a specified period.

We cannot say that these men were monks, but they created a spiritual atmosphere favourable to the development of the monastic institution when the time was ripe: people were accustomed to leaving home and city in order to dedicate themselves more completely to the search for God in solitude and silence.

This background helps to explain why the Jewish monks, the Therapeutes, established their main settlements in the desert, near Alexandria, and why St Antony, and other Christians before him, found it quite natural to retire to the desert to pray and search for the presence of God. Moreover, an acquaintance with the beauty of the Egyptian religious writings makes it less surprising to find St. Pachomius, himself an Egyptian convert, not afraid to utilize the old pagan wisdom to teach his monks.[2]

Notes

1 The relation between the Egyptian cults and monachism have been studied by F. Daumas in several articles. 'Amour de la Vie et le sens du divin dans l'Egypte ancienne', in 'Magie des Extrêmes', *Etudes*

Carmélitaines 1952; Introduction to Philo's *De Vita Comtemplativa* (ed. Le Cerf, Paris 1963); 'La Solitude des Therapeute' in *Colloques Philon,* Lyon 1966 (C. N. R. S.); 'Maitres Spirituals de L'Egypte Ancienne' in *Hermès* No. 4, 1966–67. We have summarized his conclusions and taken the quotations from the above articles.

2 Th. Lefort 'St Pachomius, Amen-em-ope. Le Museon', *t.* XI, 1927, pp. 65–74.

CHAPTER 4

The Jewish Monastic Ideal: Qumran and the *Therapeutes*

Qumran

The two centuries before Christ and the first of the Christian era were troubled times for Palestine. Foreign influences led to relaxations, infidelity to the law of Yahweh; some pious Jews, however, took a stand against these encroachments, grouping themselves into 'companies' to keep themselves free from taint.

One of these companies, belonging perhaps to the sect of Essenes, was founded by the 'Doctor of Justice' or 'Teacher of Wisdom', who was probably a 'son of Sadoc' one of the most famous of the priestly families. Documents discovered at Qumran provide us with many details of the life of this sect. Its members were scattered in the villages and formed a community as soon as they could get ten men together.

But it seems that from among these priestly and lay families there soon emerged an elite of 'willing ones' who desired to dedicate themselves to God completely and to prepare for the coming of the Messiah who, after a war lasting forty years, would conquer the world and restore the kingdom of Israel. Qumran was probably the principal centre where these chosen ones assembled to lead a communal life. The Rule is addressed only to men who must have been celibates[1] as there is no mention of women or children. But the discovery of female bones among the tombs of the large burial ground close to what we may call the 'monastery' of Qumran, perhaps indicates that the community was a double one.

The chief concern of the brethren was the scrupulous carrying out of the Law; but within the sect of the 'willing ones' another group developed, the 'pure among the pure'. Two years preparation was required to reach this state.[2] Withdrawn into the desert, they isolated themselves for God, multiplying their ceremonies of purification, and making even their meals a liturgy, thus having something in common with the Temple worship.[3]

The exterior aspects of their life were closely linked to the mentality of their age and should not hide from us the deep inward searching of these men who, both in their community life and in their personal aspirations, bore strong resemblances to Christian monks. Like the monks they believed that 'only those who turned away from wickedness were made pure' (Colu. V. 13); they sought God through a true conversion of heart and fraternal charity. The introduction to the Rule expresses well this fundamental aim:

> From the Teacher of Wisdom to all his brethren, the books of the Rule of the community. Their aim is to seek God with all their heart and soul, to do what is right and just before His face, as prescribed through the intermediacy of Moses and through all His servants, the prophets ... to bear no longer a hard and guilty heart and eyes debauched by all kinds of evil; to give entrance to all who desire to carry out the commands of God in His Covenant of grace, uniting themselves to God and living a life of perfection in His presence ... to love all the sons of light... All those who are willing to trust in His faithfulness shall bring all their intellect, their strength and their goods to the community of God. (Colu. 1:1–12)

God alone then is the head of the community, 'the God of understanding, from whom comes all that is and all that will be.' (Colu. III, 15) As the head of the sect and of the different groups they allowed only 'Stewards' charged with the interpretation of Scripture, with maintaining fidelity to the spirit of the founder, the 'Teacher of Wisdom', and with helping the members 'to walk perfectly in all the ways of God.' (Colu. III. 9) There was also a general Steward to look after the administration of goods, (Colu. IV. 20) recruitment,[4] the training of new members, and to arrange the presidency at the assemblies. (Colu. IX, 12, VI. 12) These officials were recruited only from the ranks of priests, 'Guardians of the Covenant, who seek what is pleasing to God', and to whom is revealed the meaning of the Law of Moses. (Colu. III. 9) They must have discrimination in judging character, eschewing the spirit of darkness and walking in the 'paths of light.'[5] (Colu. III. 20)

The teaching was progressive, adapting itself to each man's nature and following the stages of his progress and initiation into community life.

> These are the principles that must guide the Teacher of Wisdom in his dealings with all. He must have regard to the worth of each and the stage to which he has advanced, helping all to carry out the will of God in so far as it is step by step revealed to them, seeing that they acquire all the wisdom that is necessary at each stage ... He must assess these sons of righteousness according to their understanding and strengthen them to conform to the will of God. (Colu. IX. 12–15)

The love of what is good entails separation from all that is evil and a loathing for it, loathing that should go so far as to be a holy warfare, but it forbids that evil spirit of the heart which leads one to judge, scorn or hate one's neighbour.

> I will render evil to no man; I will seek to win man through good, for God is the judge of all the living; it is He who will apportion to each man his due. I do not strive to master the wicked in dispute before the day of retribution, but leave the iniquitous to the final judgement. (Colu. X. 17–20)

The priests were assisted in making decisions by the 'Assembly of the Many', that is, all full members or, to use modern monastic language, the professed. In the Assembly each spoke in turn, first the priests, then the elders, then the

'Many'. Members still in training could only speak with special permission:

> They will arrange themselves according to their rank, and thus assembled will take counsel together before making any decision concerning the affairs of the Many. Each shall submit the fruits of his learning to the deliberation of the community. No one must interrupt another but must wait till his neighbour has finished speaking and no-one must speak out of turn. (Colu. VI. 9–10)

The rest of the text seems to indicate that only the President of the assembly had the right to introduce a subject outside the order of the day approved by the community.

One of the chief functions of these assemblies was the admission of new members into the different stages of initiation into the community. The postulant must first be accepted by the general Steward, who, after examining him, began his instruction. He was then presented to the assembly for admission to his first year of probation, during which time he retained his possessions. There was another deliberation before admission to the second year. His possessions were then entered in the community's register, but kept apart. It was not until after a third meeting at the end of the second year that the candidate was registered as a member of the community, admitted to ritual purification, allowed to give his opinion at the assemblies and take his meals with the 'Many'.[6] (Colu. VI. 16–23)

His rank in the community was determined at his enrolment. This was not reckoned by the date of entry but by learning, merit and purity. It would be difficult today to define the criteria of such an arrangement, but it is reminiscent of the system used by Pachomius, who classified his monks according to their fervour.

The solemn oath taken at the time of enrolment gives a clear idea of the spiritual meaning of the ritual used:

> Whoever enters into the counsels of the community, binds himself by oath (in the presence of all the 'willing ones') to submit himself to the law of Moses in all that it

prescribes, with all his heart and with all his soul ... and to conform his life to the good pleasure of God.

(Colu. V. 9–10)

The individual's effort was sustained by community life, expressed in obedience, emulation in virtue and fraternal correction. The conduct commended to all new members on admission was as follows: They were reminded that they 'entered into the Covenant to be subject to one another, the lower to the higher, to search into their souls and their works; ... each should be faithful in exhorting his neighbour in humility and kindly charity towards all.'

> One should not speak to his neighbour in anger, or in complaint, or with stiff-necked harshness, or with the malice that springs from an unholy spirit. One should not hate another because he persists in error, but should give him counsel there and then and not lay oneself open to the charge of going astray with him. Likewise, no-one should introduce a subject before the 'Many' without giving previous notice of it in the presence of witnesses.
>
> (Colu. V. 23, VI. 1)

Their code of punishment again underlined the interior nature of their spiritual quest. Outward faults against the ritual are mentioned only briefly and in a general manner, (Colu. VIII. 20, IX. 2) while those that indicated an evil disposition are enumerated in detail. The heaviest sanctions were for failures in charity and faults against community life; deceit, anger, disobedience, rancour, revenge, were punished by exclusion from the council for a period of six months to a year. Murmuring against authority or calumny against one of the 'Many' meant expulsion. On the other hand, slight acts of negligence, trivial offences, or falling asleep at the council involved only ten days penance.

(Colu. VI. 24, VII. 25)

All this striving for self-mastery and fidelity to God reached its consummation in prayer.[7] Community prayer took place at sunrise and sunset: 'When the lights of heaven appeared from their holy abode and when they returned to their place of Glory.' Special solemnities took place at the new moon, at the beginning of the four seasons, on the first day of the year and during sabbatical or jubilee years.

(Colu. X. 1–2)

This connection with the course of the stars can be explained by their desire to link the earthly liturgy with that of the angels, who as they believed, controlled the movement of the heavenly bodies. Christian monks cherished this ideal of imitating the angels in a life concentrated on the presence of God, just as the men of Qumran had striven to do, to the best of their ability.

When I begin a task and at its end I will bless His Name. At coming in and going out, at sitting and at rising, and when I lie on my bed, I will exult in Him.

(Colu. X. 13–14)

Work filled the day; a third of the night was reserved for study and meditation on the Scriptures, finishing with or broken by community prayer.

Thus in its daily effort the community represented the 'remnant of Israel' withdrawn to the desert and prefiguring the final judgement. They gave praise to God in place of the blood sacrifices of the Temple to which they could not go, and in reparation for sinners; but the sect became at the same time accuser and judge of the unfaithful.

(Colu. VII. 2–7)

Once evil had disappeared, there would remain only the praise offered by the 'sons of light' standing before God on the 'eternal height'. (Hymn. III. 3) For the Rule ends naturally with a series of Hymns, full of the spirituality of the Psalms, expressing the holy aspirations of the faithful, extolling the help and grace that give sustenance and light, and finally singing the praise of the transcendent God who knows, purifies and saves the faithful:

Blessed be thou, my God,
Thou who givest understanding to the heart of thy
    servant...
and grants to the son of thy servant

To stand in thy presence for ever.

(Colu. XI. 16–17)

The *Therapeutes*

We learn of another kind of Jewish monks from the account given by Philo of Alexandria (a contemporary of Christ), in his book *De vita Contemplativa*. The most important of their communities was near Alexandria between the sea and Lake Mareotis.

The rites they observed and their spirit of fidelity to the Law and to union with God, show clearly that they belonged to the same spiritual movement as the men of Qumran. In another place Philo explicitly connects them with the Essenes. But their sociological background was very different. Instead of a persecuted sect, looking forward to a war of revenge, they lived in the peace of the rich and cultured society of Alexandria, dominated by neo-Platonic philosopy, which aspired to union with the infinite Unity.

Philo does not give us a rule but a description, written for an educated Greek elite, which has the advantages of throwing light on aspects of a life that one could only have guessed at Qumran, a life spent in liturgical prayer and search for God.

He gives us the main features of this life. A healthy position (V.C. 21–22) was chosen, isolated, not out of hatred of the world, but as providing a favourable environment for spiritual reflection. (V.C. 20) The members of the community lived in separate shacks (V.C. 24, 25, 30), they were celibates (V.C. 18, 28) the men and women were separated even for prayer (V.C. 31) and for the few meals taken in common. (V.C. 69).

All that the *Therapeutes* did was directed towards God. Every member of the sect was required:

To strive towards the sight of the Supreme Being who excels the sun in brightness, and not to abandon that state for it leads to perfect happiness. (V.C. 12)

Their very name:

> shows us what these philosophers were aiming at. They
> were called ... *Therapeutes* (and *Therapeutrides*) either
> because they practised a medicine that cared for souls in
> the grip of painful and intractable maladies, freeing them
> from the chains of pleasures, desires, afflictions,... or
> because they had learned from nature and the sacred laws
> to serve the Being who excels Goodness itself and whose
> origin dates from before the Monad. (V.C. 2)

With this end in view these aspirants, spurred on 'by celes-
tial love' ... and

> by a passionate longing for an immortal and blessed life,
> left their possessions to their sons or daughters or other
> relatives, willingly renouncing their heritage while still
> alive. (V.C. 12–13)

Probably their families were charged with providing a
modest pension for them, so that they need not work and
could devote all their energies to the quest for 'spiritual
riches'. So, 'stripped of their possessions, they left forever
brothers, children, wives, fathers and mothers ... and the
land of their birth.' (V.C. 18) to avoid the temptation of
ever again involving themselves in wordly affairs.
   During the whole week they remained in solitude, usually
in the place set apart for prayer:

> In each dwelling there was a sacred place called the sanc-
> tuary... Here they practised the mysteries of their holy
> life in solitude. They took nothing with them, no food, no
> drink, but only copies of the laws, the Oracles of the
> Prophets, hymns and other books, to help them to
> increase and perfect their devotion and knowledge. God
> was always present in their minds; even in their dreams
> they imagined nothing but the beauty of the divine
> perfections and powers. (V.C. 25–26)

This attentiveness to God was nourished by the regular

regime of study, prayer, meals:

> It is customary to pray twice a day, in the morning and in
> the evening. At day break they ask for the light of heaven
> to shine in their minds, and on retiring they pray that the
> soul, withdrawn as it were, into its council chamber, may
> devote itself to the search for truth. (V.C. 27)

After having thus meditated in solitude during the week,
they assemble on the Sabbath for community prayer:

> They sit according to age, in a becoming manner, keeping
> their hands under their habits ... Then the oldest and
> most versed in their teachings advances to address them.
> His look and voice are firm; he speaks with logic and
> understanding, expressing his ideas with precision and
> explaining them in detail; the discourse thus penetrates to
> the depths of the soul where it remains firmly established.
> The large sanctuary where they assemble on the seventh
> day is an enclosure divided into two parts, one for the
> men, the other for the women. For it is the custom for the
> women also to come to listen. They are filled with the
> same zeal and lead the same life as the men. The two
> groups are separated by a fairly high wall, so that the
> women can maintain a suitable reserve and yet hear what
> is said. (V.C. 29–33)

Meals and clothing are marked with the same restraint:

> No one eats or drinks before sunset because they judge
> that, if philosophic pursuits are worthy of light, the needs
> of the body, on the contrary, belong to darkness. (V.C.
> 34) They eat no costly food but ordinary bread seasoned
> with salt; the most delicate add hyssop to it. Their drink
> is spring water. Their clothing is very commonplace... In
> winter they wear a thick mantle of shaggy skin, in
> summer a slave's tunic or light garment... In short, they
> practise modesty and simplicity. (V.C. 38–39)

It is noticeable that the bread was made from leaven flour

out of respect for the temple where only unleavened bread was used. Ordinary meals, it seems, were taken in the solitude of the cell, but the Sabbath of the seventh week was a festival day. There was a common liturgical meal. It began with a homily given by the President;[8] this was followed by chants; then the novices set the table and served. There were no slaves for 'owning servants is contrary to nature, by which we were all born free.' (V.C. 70)

> The meal is followed by a sacred vigil ... All rise and arrange themselves in two choirs, one of men and one of women ... Then they sing hymns in God's honour ... sometimes in unison, sometimes answering in harmony, and accompanying themselves with action and dancing. Then, inspired by zeal, they sing in strophe and antistrophe, either forming a procession or remaining in their places ... (V.C. 83–94)

At dawn, morning prayer was said at the same time, and each 'withdrew to his sanctuary to apply himself again to the study of philosophy'. (V.C. 89) And Philo concludes:

> Citizens of heaven and of earth, they are truly united with the Father and Creator of the universe through the virtue that brought them into friendship with God. (V.C. 90)

The sectaries of Qumran and the *Therapeutes* were contemporaries of Christ and the Apostles. Reading these texts lends a new colour to the account given in Acts of the life of the first Christian community in Jerusalem:

> And they were persevering in the doctrine of the Apostles and in the communion of the breaking of bread, and in prayers ... All they that believed were together and had all things in common. They sold their possessions and goods and divided them to all, according as everyone had need. (Acts II. 42–45)

Knowledge of these Jewish monks helps us to understand how this passage from Acts became one of the principal sources of Christian monachism. All the Fathers of the early centuries, moreover, believed that the *Therapeutes* were Christian, for as Eusebius of Caesarea says, this account of Philo 'manifestly contains the rules of the Church which are still observed among us.' (Hist. Eccle. II. XVII. 1–2) There is no historic proof of any direct connection between these movements of pious Jews and the disciples of Jesus; but can we suppose that John the Baptist in the desert was completely ignorant of the Qumran community? And when Clement, who knew Philo and adopted his methods, praises the advantages of a life of solitude for God, in this same Alexandria a few years later, can we assume that the belief of the Fathers was based on nothing but theory?

Notes

1 The text of the Rule is written in several columns. The references give the number of the column, followed by that of the line in *Les Textes de Qumran*, transl. by J. Carmignac and P. Guilbert, Paris, 1961. According to the Law, marital intercourse involved ritual impurity, cf. *Ex.* 19, 15; *Lev.* 15, 18; *1 Sam.* 21, 14.

2 In its search for ritual purity, this sect has much in common with the Hindu social system, dominated by the priestly Brahmin caste. A strange number of similarities are apparent as, for instance, cooking done by members of the highest caste, and even keeping the left hand for less noble uses which would make it unfit to carry out more worthy acts. This helps to account for the fact that among the first converts of the Judeo-Christian missionaries in India, the majority were Brahmins.

3 A notable feature of the Essene cult was their break with the sacrificial worship of the Temple, which was an essential part of Jewish life. As they could not go to the Temple, they made instead a sacrificial offering of praise and of acts pleasing to God. cf. O. Betz: 'Le ministère cultuel à Qumran', in *Recherches Bibliques* IV.

4 The text does not state clearly whether the functions of President of the Assembly, Steward, and master of novices might be fulfilled by the same person.

5 The attribution of all influences, good and evil, to spirits who fight for man's heart is a doctrine that the Jews probably picked up during their exile in Persia. It was to re-appear among the Christian monks of Syria, who also had contact with Persia, and before them among the Judeo-Christian writers such as those of the *Didache* and the *Epistle to Barnabas*.

6 The commitment was final; to go back was considered a blameworthy weakness. If anyone left of his own accord, he could be

received back but only after undergoing again the two preparatory years. To leave after ten years membership was a 'betrayal' and made return impossible, as would be the case if one were expelled for a serious fault. (Colu. VI. 17–25)

7 The 'monks' of Qumran must have followed the traditional Jewish custom of prayer thee times a day, with additions of their own. cf. K. Hruby: 'Les heures de la prière dans le Judaisme à l'époque, de Jésus' in *La prière des heures* by Mgr. Cassien and D.B. Botte, Paris 1963, *Lex Orandi 35*, pp. 59–84.

8 The numbers refer to the *De Vita Contemplativa* edited by P. Géoltrain in *Semitica* X, 1960, quoted V.C. followed by the number of the paragraphs.

CHAPTER 5

Contacts between the East and Christian Monasticism

It is certain that Christian monasticism developed according to its own logic in the perspective of the Gospel, but the world in which it was born had contacts with Asia, and monks, like everyone else, are influenced by the idea of their times.

The first noticeable contacts are the similarities observed by specialists[1] between certain Greek pre-Christian writings and Buddhist and Jain texts. Pyrrho of Elis, the founder of the school of sceptics, who visited India with the armies of Alexander in 327 BC, began to teach ideas that he must have borrowed from the East, on his return, for they seem to have no precedent in Greek literature. Some of these views are in accordance with the Bible and were stressed by Christian monks, for instance, the importance of freedom from the passions, the purification of the soul and the acquisition of a balanced mind to attain supreme Peace, or again, the essential distinction between appearances and ultimate reality. These truths were, at that period, being taught by the Jains; they were developed later in the texts of the primitive Mahayanist literature, such as the *Prajnaparamita*. This same work has amazing similarities with the Gnostic and neo-Platonic writings in the central role assigned to Wisdom. This is found again in the later books of the Old Testament; it was applied to Christian mysticism by Origen and by many others after him.

It is equally interesting to note that Clement of Alexandria states,[2] without fear of contradiction, that the Greek philosophers had borrowed their ideas from pagan sages, among whom he names explicitly Hindu, Jain and Buddhist ascetics.[3]

Beyond these occasional influences, an important current of thought and ascetic practice moved around the Middle East between the 1st century B.C. and the 4th century A.D. Its origin seems to be Indian, since it bases itself on a dualism which extolled a detachment from the material world, something which was professed by the Jains and other Hindu ascetics.

One can also find traces of this, a little before Christ, among the Essene Jews who retired to the desert to live a life of asceticism and prayer. At that time the practice began of giving a baptism of repentance, such as was given by Saint John the Baptist.

At the end of the 2nd century, Saint Irenaeus and Saint Clement of Alexandria found themselves in opposition to groups of Christians who called themselves 'Encratites' and wanted to impose celibacy and abstinence from meat and wine on everyone. These practices were usual among the Hindu monks, and among the Christians they derived from a spirit of detachment from matter which was considered to be evil. These ideas were the source of various heresies combatted by the fathers of the Church right up to the 4th century.

In the 2nd century, Mani founded in Persia the religion which bears his name – Manicheism – which itself has a strongly dualistic base.

In 4th century Syria, the gate of the West facing India, we find some Christian monks who used the typical practices of their Hindu counterparts: a life of wandering, living under a tree, no use of fire, etc.

All these indications show that Christian monasticism was born and given its first structures in a time and place much influenced by the East, in particular by India. In these societies, asceticism and escape into the desert were, for different reasons, considered as part of normal life. This does not imply a direct doctrinal dependence on other religions, but it certainly helped the development of a Christian monasticism.

Notes

1 See, for example, E Couze, *op. cit.* p. 140 ff 'Parallels'. The comparisons made by a Vöölbus in *History of Monachism in Syriac Orient*, between this monachism and the heretical or semi-pagan ascetical currets of the time are interesting but often tenuous and contested by other specialists.

2 Clement of Alexandria *Stromata* 1:15; 71:3–6.

3 For the sake of uniformity with the chapter on Hinduism, we have used Sanskrit words for the technical terms.

Part Two
Christian Monasticism

CHAPTER 6

History

1. ORIGINS

The first centuries

Christianity appeared as a religion endowed with such a dynamism that it managed in three centuries to overcome the extreme immorality and tyranny of the time despite many bloody persecutions. Love for Christ was the hidden spring of this wonderful change. It was shown at first by the martyrs but later by those who dedicated their whole life to Christ. For his sake men and women, even sometimes entire families decided to live a life of perfect continence. In the primitive Church consecrated Virgins and *Continentes* were revered as a special category from the first century onwards, and by the end of the second century we find in Tertullian allusions to a ceremony of consecration of Virgins as Brides of Christ. They led a life of prayer, fasting, retirement and good works, individually at home or in small groups generally living on the outskirts of the towns. At the same time the first doctors of the Church: Clement of Alexandria (+ 215) and Origen (+ 253) in the East, Tertullian (+ 220) and St. Cyprian (+ 258) in the West, praise asceticism. They describe the control of one's thoughts and passions as a necessary condition for one's purification and dedication to God, which in turn enable one to receive the light of the Word of God and the power to love Him. Virginity consecrated to God realises in the soul the union of Christ with the Church and replaces martyrdom as the way to give oneself to God.

After the persecutions

So we cannot be surprised to see that, as a reaction against the easy way of life brought to Christians by the Constantinian peace, the lofty ideal advocated by the Fathers received a fresh impulse. With a common aim of union with God by love, in prayer and meditation, in universal charity and unworldliness, several ways of living will be practised: some remained in the town near the sanctuaries developing the liturgical prayer, others went alone seeking God in the solitude and majestic silence of the desert and yet others organized the cenobitic life.

2. THE GREAT FOUNDERS OF THE FOURTH CENTURY

The monastic movement in Christianity at the end of the persecutions was an original and spontaneous phenomenon appearing simultaneously in the whole Christian world. Though it did not derive from any non-Christian monasticism, it took different shapes according to the local religious cultures.

Syria

From an Indian point of view the history of the Christian monastic development should begin with Syria. The regular trade between the two countries favoured mutual cultural and spiritual influence. Later, Syriac monks will bring Christianity to India; but the first Syriac Christian ascetics borrowed quite naturally many practices from Indian monasticism, especially that of the monks wandering and begging. At that time the people of Syria were intent on an extremely radical asceticism; they practised penances like carrying chains, living under a tree or at the top of a pillar like the famous St Simon Stylites. But we know, through the lives of these monks written by Theodoret of Cyrus in his *History of the Monks*, that these practices were not considered by contemporaries as eccentricities; they were in

harmony with the local milieu. At a deeper level we find
also an Indian influence in the stress on personal prayer, on
the 'taste of God' experienced in the depth of the heart. It is
in this milieu that some of the most delicate monastic
writers of the East flourished. The first of them, St Ephrem
(+ 373), poet and liturgist, had the merit of pointing out the
essentials of monastic life. 'What makes a monk is not
simply to live in a forest but to master heart and mind, to
practise unworldliness, assiduous prayer and above all
charity.'[1] But this primitive Syriac monasticism received
very soon the impact of the Egyptian and Cappodocian
monastic traditions whose origins are better known.

Egypt

St Antony

In Egypt, St Antony (251–356) is one of the first, and in any
case, the most famous of the hermits. His life, written by St
Athanasius, Bishop of Alexandria, presents him as the
athlete of Christ having by his continual struggle and his
faithfulness to grace reached the perfect self-mastery. He
approached the full harmony existing before Adam's fall in
man's faculties and in his relations with God and with his
fellow men. After twenty years of seclusion in an aban-
doned fort, at the request of a crowd of visitors,

> he went out as from a sanctuary where he had conse-
> crated himself to God and had been filled with the Holy
> Spirit; his face was neither too glad nor too stern, he
> showed neither displeasure at seeing himself surrounded
> by such a crowd, nor complacence at being greeted and
> venerated by so many people, but he was in everything of
> an admirable equanimity and peace of mind, he showed
> indeed that he was ruled by nothing but reason ... God
> gave so much strength and sweetness to his words that he
> comforted all who were afflicted, telling that there is
> nothing in the world better than to love Christ[2].

To his disciples he recommended that they should fight

against negligence up to their last breath, beginning again and again every morning. Virtue is not an extraordinary thing, for to have an upright heart is nothing else than to keep one's soul in the same purity as when it was created.[3]

St Antony's life had a tremendous influence and attracted thousands of souls to monastic life. He was himself living usually in the depths of the desert, but he came out at regular intervals to receive the crowds of visitors asking his spiritual advice. As a true hermit he never kept more than one or two brethren with him but had many solitary disciples having more or less regular contacts with him. One of them was a young student at Alexandria, Hilarion, recently converted to Christianity, who later on came back near Gaza, his birth place, to establish there monastic life both for hermits and for cenobites.

The Desert Fathers

Around 330 another solitary, St Amoun, was helped by the advice of St Antony to arrange for his disciples a semi-eremitic way of living where monks dwelt in solitary cells scattered in the desert around a central church where they gathered on Sundays. He established at first a centre at Nitria on the border of the desert, south-west of Alexandria and a few years later, for the lovers of solitude, *The Cells* a little further in the desert. At the same time St Macarius the Egyptian founded in the deep desert, 40 miles in the South the still existing monastic centre of Scete.

The *Lausiac History* of Palladius, the *Historia Monachorum in Egypto* and the *Sayings of the Fathers* tell us the story of the great Desert Fathers: Pior, Pambo, Or, Macarius of Alexandria, Evagrius at Nitria and the Cells; Ammoes, John Colobus, Isidore and Paphnutius at Scete along with Poemen who probably was the first to begin the collection of the *Sayings of the Fathers* whose wisdom and virile spirituality have been throughout the centuries one of the main sources of the monastic tradition. The Desert Fathers specialized in the study of the passions of the human heart. An elder said: 'The monk's work is to see his thoughts coming from far away'.[4] They wanted to master them in order to get the perfect tranquillity or *apatheia* required for contemplation. This process was described at length with its various stages by Evagrius who discovered also the eight principal vices from which the seven deadly sins are derived.

The spirituality of the desert admitted two divergent aspects. The first is represented by Arsenius, a former tutor of the Emperor's sons, austere and silent, closing his door to visitors; his motto: 'flee, keep silent, be in peace' echoed in the whole East. On the other hand we have the always gentle and smiling Moses, the tall black Ethiopian, a converted brigand, comforting all those who were coming to see him. To a brother who said when taking leave 'Forgive me, Father, for I prevented you from following your rule', the old man answered: 'My rule, brother, is to comfort you peacefully when you come, and then to send you home with charity.'[5]

The influence of Scete was spread far and wide by monks trained there, who founded monastic centres in other countries. One of the most famous was established on Mt. Sinai by Abba Silvanus around 380.

St Pachomius

Besides the semi-eremitic centres numbering from a few individuals to several hundreds of monks, we see, still in Egypt during the same period, the creation of a highly organized type of cenobitic life. This development was due to a young pagan, Pachomius (293–346), led to Christ by the charity of some Christian villagers giving food to destitute prisoners. He placed mutual obedience and fraternal charity as the corner-stones of his monasteries:

He was a herdsman close to the great Good Shepherd, Christ, ... He was going quite often from monastery to monastery to visit the brothers, warning them all by the word of God, like a nursing mother warning her children by the affection of her heart.[6]

At his death, ten years before Antony, his monasteries were

organized in a kind of Congregation grouping several thousands of monks.

Asia Minor

St Basil

In Asia Minor the primitive groups of ascetics developed in small and very austere communities. In 356, the year of St Anthony's death, a young lawyer, St Basil (330–379), entered one of them. Later on he was ordained priest and then elected Bishop and, as such, was consulted by the numerous monastic groups of his diocese. He searched for the answers through meditation on the Scriptures. Trying simply to apply their teaching to monastic life he gave it its main scriptural basis. Several collections were made of these answers which are also called his *Rules* and were soon spread all over the Christian world. On the local level his main effort was to integrate into the Church the dynamism of men who were often stirred up by the heretical or non-Christian currents of the time. Their zeal should not be quenched but

> quickened by passionate, insatiable, unshakable, immutable desire of God. This disposition will be ordained by an intelligent and persevering contemplation of the greatness of God's glories and by a continuous and thankful remembering of the benefits we received from him.[7]

He insisted also on moderation and on the duty of charity among the brethren and with outsiders.

St Gregory of Nyssa

St Gregory of Nyssa (+394) Basil's younger brother completed his work by developing the mystical aspect of his asceticism. The writings of the two brothers remain the basis of the Eastern monachism and have had a great influence in the West up to our days.

St John Chrysostom

Another Doctor of the Church St John Chrysostom (+ 407) had something of an intuition of the future diversification of the religious orders: he invited those living in the towns to be, for the faithful of each generation, a model of Christian life and a sign of Christ's Incarnation and presence. On the other hand he acknowledged the value of the solitary life and gave precision to its function in the Church: 'Monks contribute to the salvation of their fellow-men, helping by their penances and their prayers those who are in charge of the Church.'

Syria

Macarius

At the same time arose in Syria the so-called Macarius, a great but unknown writer, whose works were attributed to the famous Egyptian hermit. His *Spiritual Homilies* are in close connection with the writings of St Gregory of Nyssa. He accomplished in Syria a work St Basil did in Cappadocia: he purified and gave to the Church what was valuable in Messalianism and other spiritual trends of his time. The themes he develops – the Holy Spirit giving to the soul the illumination of Christ's light, prayer as the monks' principal activity and the constant warfare between good and evil in men's hearts – are the source of some of the main characteristics of Eastern monastic spirituality.

The first monastic missions

Another character impressed on the Syriac monachism by persecutions and by the semi-nomadic life of the local population is its love of travel or exile from one's country for God. It led monks, following the caravans, to found Churches in Arabia, Persia, India, Central Asia and even up to China. Syrian monks are also responsible for the introduction of the monastic life at Constantinople around 380. By its geographical position Syria is also the north gate of Palestine for

European pilgrims. Passing through they visited the local ascetics; Theodoret speaks of groups of Britons consulting St Simon Stylites. It is probably through these pilgrims that the Syriac influence was to be felt soon in the West.

Palestine

In the Desert

St Chariton played in Palestine a role similar to Anthony's, his contemporary in Egypt. Drawn to the desert near the Dead Sea by the persecutions he lived there an eremitic life which attracted many disciples to him. But as a lover of solitude he entrusted his monks to the care of one of them and went deeper into the desert. Before leaving

> he established what is convenient for monastic life: to stop eating before hunger be satisfied, to make psalmody and prayer in day time and at night, to avoid idleness the cause of many evils, to do manual work which should be irrigated by the holy psalms

He was thus at the origin of a genuine monastic organisation the *Laura*: a church, often in a cave, with a cluster of cells used for the training of the newcomers, and, further in the desert, solitaries who came back once a week to the centre for the Sunday liturgy and for taking provisions for their frugal meals and for their work of making mats or ropes.

At Jerusalem

In the Holy places themselves, especially on Mt. Sion and Mt. Olivet monastic colonies seem to have existed very early, formed in the majority of cases by foreign visitors desirous to settle there, either in cells scattered on the mountain or in cenobitic groups of monks and of nuns. Among these pilgrims were several ladies of high rank and St Jerome who in 386 founded at Bethlehem a monastery for men and another for nuns.

Europe

The precursors

Indeed monastic life had also developed in the West: in the second half of the third century there were hermits and small groups in the solitude of the Mediterranean islands. Others lived near a sanctuary or were formed into a community by a holy bishop like St Eusebius at Vercelli (+371), St Ambrose at Milan (+397), and St Hilary at Poitiers (+367). Elsewhere some rich men desirous of an austere Christian life, like St Sulpicius Severus (+420) and his friend St Paulinus of Nola (+431), established ascetic communities in some of their estates. This first Western monachism was early influenced by the Egyptian Fathers, mainly through St Athanasius of Alexandria; indeed it is worth noticing that he wrote his life of St Antony at the request of the Western ascetics he had met during his exile in Europe.

St Martin

The first monk to become famous in the West is St Martin (+397). Son of a Roman military officer, himself a soldier in his youth, disciple of St Hilary, after some years of eremitical and communal life he was elected bishop of Tours. He organized near his episcopal see a kind of Laura and in his innumerable missionary journeys in Gaul he inspired the formation of a number of monasteries and hermitages. His life, written by Sulpicius Severus, had an influence comparable to that of St Antony by St Athanasius. It is to him that St Benedict dedicated the oratory he built on Monte Cassino.

St Jerome

In contrast to Martin, the simple man preaching to the half-barbarian populations of the West, two highly cultured men representing the best of the old Roman civilisation will bring an important contribution to the monastic life: St Jerome whom we have met at Bethlehem (+420), was a scholar. He lived a monastic life, at first in Syria and then came back to Italy, where he was the secretary of Pope Damasus. Then he visited the main monastic centres and finally settled at Bethlehem, consecrating his life not only to his famous translations and commentaries on the scriptures, but writing and translating for the West the life and works of the holy Eastern monks.

St Augustine

The other is St Augustine (+430). Former professor at Rome, Carthage and Milan, he was converted under the influence of St Ambrose and founded a monastery first at his native place, Thagaste in North Africa, then near his episcopal see at Hippo. His monachism is nearer to the primitive urban monastic groups than to the Desert Fathers. He is a seeker of God, truth, love and beauty, and in his Rule he takes as his model the fraternal love in prayer and detachment of the primitive Church at Jerusalem. From him the Western monks will take the ideals of common life and mutual charity leading to the love of God.

3. THE FIRST DEVELOPMENTS OF MONASTIC SPIRITUALITY

The Mystics of the 5th Century

In the third and fourth centuries, monastic life had spread all over Christendom; it will now reach its full development and flourish in an abundant literature, despite the great misfortune of the time, coming from the Barbarian invasions and the doctrinal upheaval of the Christological heresies.

The two names to be mentioned first are Mark the Hermit and Diadochus of Photice. Both lived in the first half of the fifth century, Mark in Galatia, the other as a monk and later bishop of Photice in Epirus. They followed the path of the so-called Macarius, insisting on the experimental character of spiritual life but stressing that baptism is its basis. *Ascesis* is understood by them as a means of reaching by steps the full flowering of baptismal grace.

A few years later the Pseudo-Dionysius, probably a Syrian monk, made the greatest effort attempted by a Christian to make use of the Neo-Platonic philosophy while keeping the essentials of the Christian orthodoxy. For him monastic life should be 'unified in a concentration exclusive of any diversion, to lead monks to the divine monad and to the perfection of the love of God'.[8]

Foundations and first monastic writings in Syria and Palestine

In Syria there also took place the foundation of an important monastery at the tomb of the hermit St Maro (+410) from which are derived the Maronite monks who remained steadfast in the Chalcedonian faith when most of the other monasteries of Syria and Persia became Monophysite.

The growing insecurity of the Egyptian deserts, due to the Arab raids, forced the monks to emigrate elsewhere, founding new monasteries on the seashore near Alexandria or far away in Palestine and in Ethiopia. The few who remained, grouped their cells near the Church inside a fortified enclosure. It is to preserve the memory of the golden age of the great Desert Fathers that their *Life and Sayings* were collected and spread by the emigrants all over the East. Later Theodoret wrote his *History of the Monks* and Cyril of Scythopolis the *Life of the Saints of the desert of Judaea*.

The Palestine of the fifth century witnessed the main development of the *Lauras*. It was started by St Euthymius (+437) a gifted ecclesiastic who, fleeing popularity, became a hermit in St Chariton's *Laura*. His holy life not only attracted disciples for whom he founded half a dozen *Lauras*, but converted Arab tribes which he organized in a fervent Church with its own hierarchy. He was like a Father to the Palestinian Church, its light in the doctrinal controversies, and many of his disciples were chosen as bishops or to occupy leading positions among the clergy.

His disciple St Sabas (+532) continued his work and gave the final touch to the organisation of the Lauras. His main foundation the *Great Laura* or *Mar Saba Laura* will play an important role in the monachism of the following centuries and has survived up to our days the stormy periods of persecutions, invasions and Islamic domination.

At the end of the sixth century we find there John Moschus the author of the *Spiritual Meadow* a collection of interesting Stories and Sayings of monks of this time. Sabas and his successors, though they lived in the desert, day and night, praying in solitude, were not indifferent to the needs of their contemporaries. They used the abundant gifts they received to build alms-houses in the towns; by their advice and writings they fought victoriously for orthodoxy and we find them even in the Emperor's palace, sent by the bishop of Jerusalem to plead for the local population.

The First Monastic Syntheses

It is also in the sixth century that the famous fortified monastery of St Catherine was built on Mt. Sinai and that its *Hegumen* St John Climacus wrote his *Ladder of Divine Ascent*, a summary of monastic spirituality that every orthodox monk is asked to read during Lent.

The region of Gaza at the junction of Egypt and Palestine was the providential place for the realisation of the first and one of the best syntheses of monastic asceticism and spirituality in the lively, well balanced and wonderfully simple Conferences and Letters of Dorotheus of Gaza (+ c.570).

At Constantinople monachism develops in the fifth and sixth centuries mainly through monks coming from Egypt and Syria. Under the Emperor Justinian (+565) there were eighty monasteries in the city. One of them practised the *Ceaseless praise*: the monks were divided in several batches replacing each other in the choir so that the divine office was said day and night without interruption; hence their name of *acemetes*, (not sleeping).

The same Justinian is also responsible for a special kind of monastic literature: the legislation which tends to impose uniformity on all the monasteries. But this tendency will never be fully dominant in the East because of the contradictory trend, mainly Syriac in its origin, toward the spiritual freedom of eremitism and of extreme corporal penance.

The First Rules in the West

The influence of the Eastern writers was not confined to their own countries. Latin translations made them soon accessible to Western readers: part of St Basil's Rules (the *Small Asceticon*), the Pachomian writings, the *History of the monks in Egypt*, several collections of the *Sayings of the Fathers* and the *Lausiac History* of Palladius. But a more original writer who was mainly responsible for introducing Eastern monastic doctrine in the West is Cassian (+435) who visited Palestine and spent about 15 years as a monk in Egypt. His *Institutions* and *Conferences* are a remarkable exposition of the observances and doctrines of the Egyptian monks, particularly that of Evagrius. They form a corpus of asceticism and spirituality both quite traditional and well adapted to the Western monasteries, which were multiplying at the same time in Italy, France and Spain. The most important of them was that of Lerins situated in a small Mediterranean island near the French coast. It followed the pattern of the Oriental *Lauras* where monks, after their training in a central monastery, lived a semi-eremitic life in cells scattered around in the solitude.

New Rules are made for these monks and for nuns by synods of Abbots like the two *Rules of the Holy Fathers*, the *Rule of Macarius*, by Abbots like Fructuosus of Braga and Martin of Dumes, or by Bishops like Caesarius (+542) and Aurelian of Arles (+551), Leander (+600) and Isidore of Seville (+636). But the longest and the most important of them is the *Regula Magistri* which is the first in the history to make an attempt to codify in an orderly way the whole life of a monastery.

St Benedict

It is in this context that the *Rule of St Benedict* appears which puts in the framework of the *Regula Magistri* the best of the Eastern and Augustinian traditions, chosen with a genial discretion and adapted to the local conditions. Benedict (+ c.550) himself lived in Italy. As a young man he studied in Rome but, dismayed by the low moral standards of his environment and 'desirous to please God alone', he fled the city and 'retired to a deserted spot called Subiaco'. There he spent several years in a cave 'alone under the eye of God'. Later on 'as he had gathered many disciples around him for the service of the almighty God he was able ... to build twelve monasteries, in each of them he set an Abbot and twelve monks'. After some years he founded a more important house at Monte Cassino near Naples. Besides his genius for discerning the main values and making the synthesis of the monastic tradition, Benedict was a man of wise moderation and great charity, penetrated by a deep sense of contemplation and reverence of God.

We owe these details to his Life, written some years after his death by Pope St Gregory the Great (+604) who included it in his *Dialogues*. With his *Morals on Job* they express an ideal of monastic life fully oriented towards contemplation and 'quiet in God', which had a deep influence on the Medieval monastic spirituality.

The British Isles

We have to return now to the beginning of the fifth century to see the first steps of British and Irish monasticism. It was certainly influenced by the way of life of the Eastern monks: we met pilgrim Britons at the feet of St Simon Stylites and it is a fact that the primitive Celtic monachism has much in common with the Syriac tradition of extraordinary penances, eremitism, travel for God. It seems that the actual starting of the monasteries was due to the Missions of continental bishops who, like St Germain of Auxerre spread the influence of Lerins. St Germain was succeeded by holy local disciples. These were generally at the same time Abbots and Bishops, who founded many monasteries: St Pol, St Gildas, St David in Wales with St Samson who lived in the monastery on the island of Caldey; St Patrick who went himself to Auxerre, and preached both Christian faith and monasticism in Ireland where they had a prodigious growth with monasteries containing up to 3,000 monks. From there monachism passed on to the North of England and to Scotland where it established its most famous monastic centre on the island of Iona. Some original characteristics of the Celtic monasteries will have a lasting influence in the Church: private and frequent confession, private masses, taste for literary culture and travel for God.

Travelling monks will teach their way of life on the continent and at first in Brittany where many of their countrymen had taken refuge against the invasion in England of the pagan Scots and Anglo-Saxons. The most famous of these pilgrim monks was St Columbanus (+615) who wrote a very austere Rule and founded monasteries in Burgundy, Switzerland (St Gall), and North Italy. But in his turn, in 596, St Gregory the Great sent to England St Augustine, future archbishop of Canterbury, with 40 Roman monks for the evangelisation of the pagan invaders.

4. MONACHISM AT THE TIME OF THE ISLAMIC EXPANSION

In the midst of dramatic events

While Columbanus and Augustine were striving to establish monasteries among the Northern invaders of Europe, dramatic events were on their way at the other end of the Christian world. In 622 a new Arab Prophet moved with his followers from Mecca to Medina. Mohammedanism was born. In a few decades it conquered all the Eastern and Southern shores of the Mediterranean Sea, reduced Christian monastic life in these countries to a few isolated points and cut off for centuries the Western monasticism from its Eastern roots.

The seventh century saw in Egypt and Palestine the sad spectacle of the end of the Christian era. Jerusalem, already taken by the Persians in 614, fell into the hands of the Muslims, headed by Caliph Omar, in 638, and Alexandria underwent the same fate in 642. After a period of relative tolerance monasteries were finally sacked, monks killed or dispersed.

Liturgy and spirituality progress in Egypt and Palestine

A few centres remained like Scete, St Sabas' *Laura*, St Catherine on Sinai, all enclosed in the high walls of a fortress. But behind these walls spiritual and intellectual life continued. It was at Mar Saba that the writings of *Isaac of Niniveh* were translated from Syriac into Greek. Though a Nestorian Bishop, Isaac developed all the traditional themes of the monastic literature from a knowledge derived both from the study of the Bible and from personal experience which was to assure the extraordinary success of his writings in all the Mediterranean world. Sabaite monks played also an important role in the creation of the Orthodox hymnody and liturgy. During the seventh and eighth centuries the *Great Laura* was illumined by many saints, mystics and theologians who fought for the keeping of the holy Ikons; the greatest of them was St John Damascene (+754).

On Sinai, monks, following the trend of the so-called Macarius and Diadochus of Photice developed the spirituality of the 'keeping of the heart' and of the 'Jesus prayer': 'Jesus, Son of God, have mercy on me a sinner' repeated endlessly from the depths of the heart. Meanwhile they continued the theological controversy with monophysites and begin to refute Islam.

Only on the High mountains of Ethiopia, aloof from the main ways of the Arabian invaders, monachism coming from Egypt and Syria continued its development and contributed greatly to the conversion of this country to Christianity (Monophysite).

Byzantine Monachism takes its definite characters

In Syria, the Maronite monks persecuted by both the Arabs and Jacobites emigrated to Lebanon and established their centre in the Holy Valley (Qadisha) near Tripoli. But it was the Bythinian monasteries of Mt. Olympus and St Auxentius – still at this time in Byzantine territory – which were at this period the brightest light of monachism. Their mystics fostered the two main currents which will characterize the

Byzantine monasticism. The first was represented by St Maximus the Confessor (+662), a remarkable theologian who studied the divinisation of our human nature by its union with Christ. In the same line, the taste of many holy hermits for poverty and solitary contemplation flowered in the *hesychast* spirituality, favouring continuous prayer in the interior silence of a solitary life. But in reaction against the errors of an eremitism, adopted without proper training, there appeared a second current with St Theodore the Studite who organized a strict cenobitic life taking its inspiration from Basil, Pachomius and Dorotheus of Gaza. Byzantine and Slav monachism received a lasting influence from the Studite monks.

If St Theodore speaks mainly to his religious of fraternal charity and of the self mastery leading to the interior peace, it is another Studite St Symeon the New Theologian who will be the greatest mystic of the Byzantine Church. He developed the tradition of the prayer of Jesus and speaks openly of his own spiritual experience in a manner heralding that of the best Western mystics.

Finally it is during the ninth century that hermits settled down on Mt. Athos and the first monastery was established there (963) by St Athanasius the Athonite. The *Holy Mountain* – as it is called – became and remains up to our own time the main centre of the Byzantine and Slav monachism. At the same time the Byzantine way of life developed in South Italy with Saints like St Nil who founded the community still existing in the monastery of Grottaferrata.

The difficulties caused to the Byzantine Empire by the Arabian conquests and by interior troubles impeded Eastern Monachism from extending its influence further West. Nevertheless the peace resulting from the settling down of the Northern invaders favoured the spreading of other forms of monastic life and the development of culture.

Expansion of the Benedictine Rule in Europe

Ireland and England remained the centres of expansion of monasticism and of an intellectual life based on the Bible and on the Latin classics. St Bede the Venerable (+735) was the best scholar of this time and it was his fellow country-men St Willibrord (+739) and St Boniface (+754), – followed at the next generation by St Ansgar (+865), the *Apostle of the North*, a native of Picardy – who evangelised and founded monasteries in Germany and in Northern Europe. They also worked for the reform and unification of the clergy.

In the monastic domain too they worked for unification. European monasteries generally followed a *Mixed Rule* where St Benedict's Rule was added to one or several local Rules to complete them. On account of its own value St Benedict's Rule tended to supersede the others. Ultimately these reformers requested all the monasteries to use only this Rule but they interpreted it in the light of their own Latin and Celtic background losing sight of its Eastern sources.

Charlemagne (+814) strongly supported this movement toward unity and culture. The English monk Alcuin was the main instrument in the Carolingian Renaissance: schools were reformed and the manuscripts of the Latin Classics copied in monasteries. Thanks to these monk-copyists, most of them have been preserved.

Lewis the Pious, Charlemagne's son, tried to finalise the monastic unification with the help of St Benedict of Aniane (+821). This holy man fulfilled his task by using persuasion: he wrote his *Concordia Regularum* to show the harmony which exists between St Benedict's Rule and the old local Rules. He preserved them so that the monks could profit from the tradition and see that it 'concords' with St Benedict's Rule. On the other hand, St Benedict of Aniane gave to his monasteries the traditional contemplative and liturgical orientation, nourished by the meditation of litur-gical texts and by the writings of the Fathers, especially St Gregory the Great.

Another aspect of the liturgy underwent a profound modi-fication in the eighth and ninth centuries. It was mostly the work of the monks and profoundly affected their life. The prayer of the Church had to be adapted to the joyful charac-ter of life of the new converts, inclined to exuberance, grandiose display and exteriority. Thus gradually the splendour of the worship, the duration of the office, the number of feasts, rites and ceremonies were increased. The times of silence were filled with prayers of devotion – called 'spices' by St Ansgar who felt they were useful to digest the psalms. This external splendour disappeared for a time with the decay and destruction caused by the invasions.

The Muslim Sufi mysticism

The tide of the Muslim conquests, after having occupied Spain, was reaching a Gaul already troubled by feudal anarchy and by the Norman raids. But after some years of confusion the progress of the Arabian invaders in Western Europe was arrested and Islam profited by the lull to develop its own culture. It was at this time (8th century), that the organisation of the Sufi mystics began to appear. At first regarded with suspicion by the orthodox authorities, their experience of God was integrated in the main body of orthodox theology by the great al-Gazali (+1111) and henceforth Sufism developed forming religious orders.

5. WESTERN MONASTICISM: THE BENEDICTINE CENTURIES

Monastic revival in the 10th century

In the turmoil that followed the fall of the Carolingian Empire self-sufficient monasteries could often survive when kingdoms and big estates were broken up. They became centres of life and light, diffusing what they had kept of the ancient culture and spirituality. Their unification had not been realised but the efforts of the reformers had the unexpected result of convincing monks that they all belong to a monastic family founded by St Benedict. His Rule became for three centuries the uncontested source of all European religious life.

So, despite all the political upheavals, the tenth century witnessed for the first time the movement of monastic self-reformation which now appeared spontaneously after each dark period. Holy monks following the Benedictine Rule, sometimes helped by local bishops or princes, founded fervent houses which soon became powerful centres of reform in the Church. Cluny founded in Burgundy in 910 dates first and is the most famous among many others in Gaul, Italy and the British Isles. In England the reform was led by St Dunstan (+987) and, unlike on the continent at that time, had a major part to play in the intellectual renewal of the country.

Cluny

Cluny had the rare chance to be governed for nearly three hundred years by a succession of Abbots, Odo, Mayeul, Odilo, Hugh, and Peter the Venerable who were saints, learned men and good administrators. They organized between the Mother-House and her daughters links of dependence which are at the origin of the modern religious Congregations. They placed their monasteries under the direct jurisdiction of the Pope, thus introducing the privilege of the *exemption* from episcopal control, now given to most of the religious orders.

A similar organisation was set up by many other monasteries which all together formed a net-work of Christian fervour gladly used by the reforming Papacy to counter the abuses of the time.

Taking up the ideal of St Benedict of Aniane the monks of Cluny stressed liturgy and meditation on Scripture and on the Fathers. This was to provide a good ground for a rich development in the West of monastic theology: reflection on the Christian mysteries nourished by an incessant contact with the sacred texts and enlightened by the intimate experience of the divine. St Anselm, mystical author, theologian, Abbot of the monastery of Le Bec in Normandy and finally Archbishop of Canterbury is one of the best representatives of this movement.

On the other hand monasteries, often rich and with a greater number of monks who were priests, had less need of manual work and the free time was given to the monastic liturgy. Thus gradually the splendour of the worship was increased; to the regular choir office were added prayers and psalms in honour of our Lady, of the Angels and for the dead. The Roman liturgy later borrowed a number of these monastic creations: hymns like the *Veni Creator*, *Alma Redemptoris*, *Salve Regina*, feasts like the Commemoration of the dead on the second of November, devotions like the *Way of the Cross* or the preparatory prayers for Mass attributed to St Ambrose but in reality composed by Abbot John of Fécamp.

The exuberance of the liturgy and the very prosperity of the monasteries gave rise to another movement stressing poverty, penance, silence and manual work. St Romuald (+1027) and St Peter Damian (+1072) founded Camaldoli, St Bruno, the Carthusians (1084).

Cîteaux

But the most remarkable reaction was that of Cîteaux founded in 1098. The *Charter of Charity*, written by the founders, put forth its ideal of return to the literal acceptance of St Benedict's Rule with manual work, the simple regular office with the suppression of the accretions of the last centuries. It set up also institutions of lasting influence in the Church: the General Chapter and the Canonical Visitation which proved so efficient for keeping a good observance that they would be imposed by Rome on the other religious congregations; the organisation of the lay-Brothers was also to be borrowed by many orders. The great glory of the Cistercian Order is St Bernard who gave a new impulse to monastic spirituality. Giving more attention to the Eastern Fathers – especially Origen, Gregory of Nyssa and Maximus the Confessor, known through Latin translations – he and the writers of his school fostered a mystical fervour more affective in its expression and stressing the devotion to Christ's Humanity and to our Lady.

Two other aspects of the monachism of this time are worth noting: besides the monasteries (and often in dependence on them) eremitical life was led by many silent seekers of God. On the other hand big and small monasteries worked to improve their lands in order to be able to help the poor. As a side effect they contributed efficiently to the economic development of their countries. At a higher level the great Abbots were peace-makers in the political society of their time, undertaking countless diplomatic missions for the welfare of the people and for settling quarrels among the rulers of their countries. But these social and economic results, whatever may be their material importance, remain by-products of a monachism centred before all on the search for God in prayer. It is this spiritual dynamism which little by little succeeded in uplifting the whole European society by the striving for the love of God and its natural overflow in love of men.

6.   WESTERN MONASTICISM: DECAY AND REFORM UP TO THE FRENCH REVOLUTION

Monasticism in Europe became a static rather than a dynamic spiritual power at the beginning of the thirteenth century. Dynamism passed to the recently founded Friars – Dominicans and Franciscans – then in their fresh fervour and in the glory of their success in the Universities. From another point of view it was normal that part of the all-embracing activities of the medieval monasteries should go to more specialized orders. In the following centuries this transformation gave rise to the modern active orders and enabled the monastic life to return to its fundamental contemplative vocation.

It is significant that the only monastic body to prosper in the worst period of that time (1350–1550) was that of the Carthusians, austere hermits 'never reformed and never needing reform'.

As a whole, between the Middle Ages and the French Revolution, the fortune of the European monasteries follows the ups and down of the Church in these countries. There are dark periods: the 14th century, the Hundred Years War, in the 16th the Protestant reformation and wars of religion which suppressed all the monasteries in the

North of Europe and in England, and finally, the dissolving influence of Jansenism and of the anti-religious philosophy of the 18th century.

But God raised up saints to reform and start new sprouts on the old stem of the monastic order. The Sylvestrines were founded by St Sylvester (+1267) and the Olivetans by St Bernard Tolomei (+1349). In the 15th century the monasteries organized themselves in Congregations to support each other and suppress abuses. They succeeded in founding the first monasteries in Brazil in the 16th century and, in the 17th, not only in restoring in Europe centres of eminent fervour and asceticism like the Abbey of 'La Trappe', origin of the Trappists, but also in achieving remarkable works of scholarship in the field of Patristics and history due mainly to the Congregation of St Maur.

The English monks expelled from their home-land regrouped themselves on the continent and undertook missions in England where nine of them died as Martyrs.

7. EASTERN MONASTICISM

In the Orthodox Churches

In the Middle Ages the Eastern monasteries placed mostly under Muslim domination were only allowed to persevere in their silent search for God, standing as the soul and core of the Orthodox Church which chose its bishops from among them.

But the development continued on Mt. Athos and, from there, spread to Russia under the two forms of the strict hesychastic eremitism and of the Studite cenobitism which made room for the service of the Church and of society. These tendencies are respectively represented by St Antony of Kiev (+1073) and by his disciple St Theodosius (+1074).

In the following centuries Mt. Athos continued to be the main centre of the monastic life. The cenobitic groups were still under the influence of the Studite movement but the hermits brought to light a new aspect of Hesychasm centred on the invocation of Jesus' name following the rhythm of breathing. Gregory Palamas (+1359) expounded the spiritual theology of their movement. He stressed the unity of the human being and the concomitant effect on the body of the soul's *divinisation*. It was probably under the influence of the Holy Mountain that a new start is given to Russian monachism after the Mongol invasions of the 13th century and to that of Romania in the 14th. The 15th century is one of the great eras of Russian monastic life with many foundations of monasteries and hermitages, especially in the North.

After the fall of Constantinople by the hands of the Turks (1453) monasteries of the former Greek empire were under the Muslim rule and forced to remain silent. It was nevertheless in Mt. Athos that in the 18th century the *Philocalia* was compiled, a monument of erudition and spirituality collecting the main spiritual texts of Eastern monasticism. A part of it, on the prayer of the heart, was translated into Slavonic for the use of monks of Slavonic cultures.

Indeed after a decline in the 17th and the 18th centuries, a wide-spread revival took place in Russia during the end of the 18th and the 19th century. It originated either with great monks and spiritual Masters or with holy bishops who practised monastic virtues in their dioceses. There were 550 monasteries in 1914 with more than 11,500 monks, but nearly all of them have been destroyed in the changes that followed the Revolution of 1917.

Catholic Eastern Rites

The same period saw the creation of the first monastic Congregations in the Catholic Eastern rites. The Maronite Patriarch of Antioch, Douaihi, had had the occasion to see the benefit Western monks were drawing from their organisation in Congregations, while he was studying in Europe. In 1695 he approved the constitutions of the order of the Lebanese monks of St Anthony, founded by three young Alepite monks. Some years later the order divided itself in two branches: the Alepites and the Baladites or Lebanese. In the meantime Bishop Gabriel Blauza founded the similar order of the 'Antonites of St Isaias' in 1700.

In all these congregations the houses are grouped in

Provinces and they are headed by a Superior General. The religious are trained in a monastery but some can become hermits in the neighbourhood. To the Lebanese and Antonite orders are also attached corresponding branches of nuns more or less depending on the Superior General.

The monks of the Melkite Church founded two Basilian Congregations: the Choueirites near Tripoli in 1697 and near Sidon that of St Saviour in 1708. These monks were, during the hard persecutions of the 18th century, the main support of the Patriarchate. At the same time, monastic life continued to develop in the Greek Catholic churches of Eastern Europe.

Finally the holy Armenian priest Mekitar, obliged to flee from persecution, established his congregation (Mekitarists) at Venice in 1717. Later on the congregation was divided and the new branch settled down at Vienna in 1772. Following the direction of their founder, the Mekitarists have made great achievements in publishing religious, literary and scientific works in the Armenian tongue for the intellectual and moral uplift of their fellow countrymen.

8. MODERN RENEWAL

Following the movement of the previous century new congregations were founded in the Catholic Eastern Churches: at the beginning of the 19th century that of St Hormisdas for Chaldeans whose constitutions are similar to the Maronites', and in 1829 in Lebanon the Choureites, who form a new branch of the Alepites. The hidden fervour of this monastic life is manifested by the holy life of the Lebanese Maronite monk Charbel Maklouf (+1898), canonised at the end of the Second Vatican Council and, in the Orthodox Church, by a translation in Russian of the *Philocalia* which nourished the spiritual life of the Staretz, who has a great place in the religious life of all the Slav countries.

The Marxist Revolution started an important emigration in the West, especially in America where large Orthodox Churches are now flourishing. Monasteries are being founded in Western Europe and in America. On the other hand, despite all the difficulties, monachism in the Eastern Churches still exists in the Middle East, and there has been a monastic boom in Russia, the Ukraine and Romania since 1989. Its life goes on also in Greece, especially on Mt. Athos and even develops in some parts of Central Europe and in Ethiopia.

The French Revolution and the Napoleonic wars were a severe trial to European monasticism. All the French monasteries and a great number in the surrounding countries were suppressed. But it was like a Providential pruning heralding an extraordinary new spring. Before the end of the 19th century monasteries are founded or reformed in nearly all the European countries. English monks are allowed to return home. The new foundations of Solesmes in France and Beuron in Germany start the liturgical movement. In Austria, Switzerland, Belgium, Spain, Portugal, and Italy monasteries are restored and new congregations organized which soon made foundations in North America.

These new houses flourished so much as to form by themselves several new Benedictine congregations, and, at present, American monasteries hold pride of place both in the Cistercian and Benedictine Orders.

The 20th century is also marked by the expansion of Latin monasticism in missionary countries. Beginning with South America the movement soon reached Africa and Asia. Nearly three hundred monastic houses have already appeared answering the call of the new Churches anxious to have the fulness of the Christian life present among them.

To help the reader to get a more precise idea of the strength of the monastic Orders in the world we give in Appendix I the present state of these Orders with the number of their members.

9. THE HISTORY OF NUNS

Origins

The history of nuns follows in its main lines that of the monks. They were in constant relation with each other and their bright and dark periods occurred in the same eras. Nevertheless convents or particular nuns brought such a valuable contribution to monastic life or to the Church as a whole that monasticism cannot be studied adequately without having at least a glance at the most salient aspects of their history.

The first Christian Virgins consecrated to God are found in the Apostolic times when the Acts speak of the four daughters of the deacon Philip (Acts: 21, 9). At the end of the second century Virginity is considered as a way of life acknowledged by the Church. The time of these first nuns was divided between singing psalms morning and evening, work and *Lectio Divina*, giving thus the pattern which will be followed by the first monks.

The Desert

Save for some well-to-do women, to live alone was fraught with difficulties and dangers. It explains why we find so few nun hermits in the deserts. That life required of them such a courage that Amma Sarra did not hesitate to declare, not without humour, that she was the only real man among the monks; some others found the solution of living in monks' monasteries disguised as men. Nevertheless a few convents existed before the first monasteries for we see St Antony entrusting his sister to one of them. Later St Pachomius built a house near his monastery where his sister Mary presided over 400 nuns.

Founders

It seems that the great founders associated nuns – often their own sisters – with their work. The example of St Benedict and St Scholastica is well known, St Augustine and St Caesarius had their sisters at the head of convents. In the case of St Basil it is probable that his sister Macrina was instrumental in helping him to leave the world. St Martin founded both monasteries and convents and Cassian did the same at Marseilles. By the end of the 5th century we find convents in all important towns of the East and the West and most of the Fathers of the Church wrote for their benefit treatises on Virginity. Their number grew up to the 7th century which was one of the most brilliant periods of the nuns' history.

The Golden Age

The documents of the time give us a good idea of the life in these convents. We notice at first a great freedom in the choice of the observances. Under the leadership of an Abbess the way of life took its inspiration from the various monastic writings available at that time, that is mostly those of Jerome, Augustine, the Desert Fathers, Cassian, Caesarius, Benedict and Columbanus.

Another character was the high level of culture of the nuns. Already in the 5th century we see St Jerome teaching Scripture to the learned Roman ladies grouped in his monastery in Bethlehem; but the most brilliant culture was that of England in the 7th century. St Augustine and his monks brought it from Rome to their eager new converts. Men were often too busy with wars and politics to dedicate themselves to study, so it was left to women – who occupied an important place in Anglo-Saxon society – and especially to nuns. Their convents soon became centres of intellectual and economic development and Abbesses very influential persons. Let us take St Hilda (+680) as a typical example. Daughter of a king, she founded a monastery at Whitby for the nuns and another for monks and encouraged the development of studies on Bible, art and literature. The first Anglo-Saxon poem was written by a monk of her monastery. Her wisdom was so great that no better place could be found than her monastery to hold the Council which managed to settle the difficult question of the predominance of the Latin or Celtic rite in the English Church. The learning of the English convents was brought to Germany by St Boniface who called some of their nuns to collaborate in his missionary work there. His cousin the lovely (*Die Liebe*) St Lioba (+782) had the general direction of the new German convents. She was held in such veneration that, coming once to Fulda, her companions were as usual kept outside but the monks invited her to sing with them the choir office and to share in their spiritual conference. In the following years German convents, and especially those of Canonesses, became so highly cultured that the 10th century has been called 'The Golden age for women in Germany'.

Learning

Convents spread learning through their schools: the internal school was for girls who wanted to become nuns, the external one received children coming from the best families of the country and from the neighbourhood. This choice explains the influence of the schools despite the small number of the students: no more than 10 inside and about 30 outside.

Another art cultivated in convents was the copying of manuscripts and their decoration with minatures. Many nuns, both in the East and in the West excelled in this art. It was in the English convent of Thanet that St Boniface ordered all the books he needed. (This house was refounded in 1937 with the help of German nuns.) At that time also, as in our days, nuns were skilled in the arts of needle work. Some of their Church ornaments, especially embroidery of silk with gold and pearls are among the most famous art pieces of the time.

The Dark Ages

With the 8th century the fervour of the convents seems to slacken. Against 60 nuns canonised in the 7th century, we find only 30 in the 8th and the number falls to 10 for the 9th and the 10th. A number of small convents had spread all over the Christian regions. Beside unfavourable social conditions (political troubles, Norman and Saracen raids), the small size of the communities was the main cause of the decay, for the nuns lived finally according to their fancy. To react to the situation as well as to ensure protection to the nuns, bishops encouraged them to concentrate in bigger and

more fervent houses in the towns. This movement
contributed to the development of some particular institutions.

New Institutions

That of the Canonesses grouped the isolated nuns who, as
in the first centuries, lived a pious life in their families
without the monastic observances of poverty and enclosure.
Progressively they were put under the care of an elder or
Abbess, and dwelt in one house with common refectory and
dormitory. In some way they replaced the former deaconess
helping the clergy in teaching the catechism, and caring for
the poor and the sick. They had their bright period mostly
in the 10th century in Germany but, as a whole, their easy
life was a constant cause of slackening for regular nuns.

The *Double Monasteries* already existed in the 7th
century – as we have seen in case of St Hilda; they multiplied mostly in the 9th and in the 11th centuries. They were
communities of monks and nuns living in different but
adjoining compounds under the same authority. Their
origin stemmed from two sources, either nuns taking refuge
under the protection of a monastery or the development of
a group of monks working as chaplains and helpers of a
community of nuns. In the first case both houses were under
the Abbot, in the latter the authority was in the hands of the
Abbess. The last solution seems to have worked better and
we find Congregations of Double Monasteries governed by
an Abbess up to the French Revolution. But Cluny and
Cîteaux never admitted this way of life and it declined from
the 13th century onwards.

Finally we have the *Recluses*. They lived alone in a small
cell generally built on the side of a church. The door was
sealed or walled up and they communicated with the
outside only through a small window opening inside the
church. They followed the offices of the church and spent
the rest of the time in reading, prayer and work – needle
work or copying manuscripts. Many of them were
renowned for their science, wisdom and virtue. The first
German poem owes its origin to a recluse named Ada

(+1127). Sometimes several women came to live under the guidance of the recluse and her cell had to be changed into a convent.

The Great Mystics

The monastic renewal of the 10th century gradually influenced the nuns when convents were attached to the new monastic branches, and it bore magnificent fruits in the following centuries.

The writings of St Elizabeth, nun of Shônau (+1164), are a good example of the spirituality of nuns at that time. Her book narrates her 'visions' which are a living commentary on the liturgy, and her teaching developed the traditional monastic themes: asceticism normally blossoms in mystical life, for the pure heart is filled with the divine light. Her prayer was a trustful adoration full of love, humility and patience. The radiation of this ideal on her contemporaries is illustrated by St Hildegarde (+1179) Abbess of Bingen. She had an extraordinary learning – including theology, philosophy, mysticism, medicine, natural sciences and music. She fulfilled a mission of teaching. Bishops, Kings and Princes sought her advice and by her visits, her books and her letters she played a role similar to that of St Bernard in the following century.

The 13th century is indeed that of the Cistercians. Convents of Cistercian nuns multiplied with a fantastic rapidity – several hundreds between 1200 and 1250. The influence of St Bernard reached also the monasteries and convents belonging to other monastic families and the monastic spirituality as a whole took a more affective character. It is well illustrated by St Lutgarde[9] and the three saints of Helfta: the two St Mechtilde and St Gertrude the Great.

'St Lutgarde (+1246), a Cistercian nun of Aywières; entered upon the mystical life with a vision of the pierced Heart of the Saviour and concluded her mystical espousals with the Incarnate Word by an exchange of hearts with Him.'[9]

St Mechtilde of Magdebourg (+1282) led at first a life

similar to that of St Hildegarde and retired at Helfta. She
wrote mystical books stressing the Love of Our Lord and
speaking of the Sacred Heart of Jesus. St Mechtilde of
Hackeborn (+1290) and St Gertrude (+1302) learned from
her the devotion to the Sacred Heart. They taught in their
books – especially the *Herald of the Divine Love* and the
Exercises of St Gertrude – a simple and practical spirituality
based on the divine office and the liturgy. Through rich
images they sang Jesus' love making up for our weaknesses;
they show how our Lord intervenes in the daily life of those
who trust in Him. With that they go deep into the theology
of the relations of Christ with the other persons of the Holy
Trinity. From St Mechtilde comes also the practice of recit-
ing three Hail Marys morning and evening to obtain
preservation from sin and a holy death.

The same spiritual trend was felt in the other European
countries: from the 12th to the 15th century monastic
convents in Italy gave to the Church several *Beatae* and
Saints. The best known among them are the Blessed
Santuccia Terrebotti (+1305) foundress of the Benedictine
Congregation of the Servants of Mary and St Francesca
Romana (+1440) foundress of the Benedictine Oblates.

During the same period lived in England the famous
recluse Julian of Norwich (+1414). Her book *Revelations of
Divine Love* develops the same doctrine as that of the
mystics of Helfta with less images but the same optimism
and a well balanced doctrine. Her last words were:
'Everything finishes well ... Everything is for love'.

The darkest period

But the end of the 14th century is perhaps the darkest
period of the whole history of the nuns. To the external
difficulties caused by wars, pestilence and the low morality
of the society, were added several internal causes of decay:
The nuns were again scattered in small houses without
discipline, many of them had entered without vocation
under the pressure of their families, there was no enclosure
at all and neither spiritual training nor spiritual life.

New blossom after the Council of Trent

As was the case with monks the renewal begun in the 15th century was annihilated by the Protestant Reformation which destroyed monastic life in nearly half of Europe. The Council of Trent (1545–1563) reacted by decrees stressing that entering religious life should be a free personal decision and that enclosure should be strongly enforced. Most of these regulations still standing in our days can be understood only by considering the background of that time. The reform was slowly applied but it saw a splendid upsurge in the 17th century especially in France and Italy. That fresh striving for perfection in the convents was influenced both by the mystical movement of the previous period and by the spirituality of the time stressing silent meditation, mortification and atonement, cult of the Blessed Sacrament and of the Sacred Heart. New Congregations bore the significant name of Benedictines of the Blessed Sacrament and Benedictines of Calvary. A legion of holy Abbesses reformed the convents where humble nuns reached the heights of mystical life. Typical of the time is the Blessed Jane Mary Bonomo (+1676), Abbess of Bassano near Venice. Modest and gentle in a life of suffering and humility she developed a devotion to the Sacred Heart heralding that of St Margaret Mary a few years later.

Decadence in the 18th century

Jansenism and the rationalist spirit of the 18th century withered the fervour of many souls. The abuse of music and the lack of separation between the community life of the nuns and the monastic schools introduced again the spirit of the world and slackening in many convents.

Modern revival

The bloodshed of the French Revolution (twenty nuns martyred) and the sufferings of the cold persecution of the European rationalist Sovereigns destroyed many houses. That severe pruning prepared the great revival of the 19th

and 20th centuries. Monastic life was restored in England
and in several Protestant countries. Nuns dispersed by the
Revolution refounded fervent houses and new
Congregations appeared both in Europe and in America.
The 20th century is that of the expansion in Mission territories and in some cases (Japan, Madagascar) houses of nuns
preceded or developed better than those of monks.

The character of the present spiritual trend is a return to
the monastic tradition with a balanced synthesis of the
values brought forth by the previous centuries. Bible,
liturgy and the Fathers meditated in *Lectio Divina* are
considered anew as the main sources of the spirituality;
time for silent prayer is given pride of place in the monastic
time table and guests are invited to share in the search for
God of the community. The missionary expansion with the
meeting of non-Christian cultures contributes to a return
towards a greater suppleness in the life and to an insistence
on pointing out that Union with God is the aim and specific
aspect of monastic life.

Notes

1   L. Leloir *S Ephrem* in *Théologie de la vie monastique p. 96.*
2   S Athansius *Life of St Antony*, c.7.
3   ibid. c.8.
4   H. Waddell *Sayings of the Fathers, Martin of Dumes*, 14.
5   *Martin of Dumes*, 28.
6   Th. Lefort, *Les Vies Coptes de Saint Pachome,* pp. 110–120,
    Pachomian Koinonia, Vol. 1, pp. 76–78.
7   St Basil *Short Rules*, 157.
8   R. Roques, 'Eléments pour une théologie de l'état monastique selon
    Denys l'Aréopagite', in *Théologie de la Vie Monastique*, p. 288.
9   Thomas Merton, Life of St Lutgarde, *What are these Wounds* p. IX.

CHAPTER 7

Themes of Monastic Spirituality

1. SEARCH FOR GOD

At its origin monasticism has two fundamental characteristics: it is a movement of renunciation of the world; in
that sense it is a protest against the worldliness of society
and also of Religion. But this renunciation is oriented
toward the search for a higher life, for spiritual attainment,
for an apprehension of our human nothingness and an
experience of the divine, of the Absolute. At this pre-
Christian stage of the monastic life the monk is a witness of
the highest form of religious dedication and spiritual
research. He is a seeker of the Absolute, whatever formula-
tion of it is given by the various religious traditions.

In Christianity, since its very beginning, the need was felt
for the same radical renunciation of the world and dedication to 'seeking God' as it has been practised for centuries in
non-Christian religions. The eremitism of John the Baptist
and the community life of the primitive Church of
Jerusalem as described in Acts 2, 44 are both contempora-
neous with the Essenes and are models followed by fervent
Christians since the Apostolic times. In the Church, through
the sacramental and incarnational order, the Word of God
himself led those who received it to be one with the Father,
the Son and the Spirit in their absolute transcendence.
Asceticism and virginity, appearing only sporadically in the
Old Testament, are fully acknowledged in the New. By the
middle of the third century A.D. they develop in the form of
monasticism as a powerful movement which spread all over
the Church.

The early Christian monastic movement and all the periodical reforms in the past are intimately associated with the same radical approach of world renunciation and dedication to the search for God. Remarkable in this respect are Gregory of Nyssa in the East and Gregory the Great in the West, and right through the Middle Ages up to our own days this quest for God blossomed into lives wholly prompted by a burning desire for God. This remains the proper charism of the monastic life in the Church. It has recently been brought into a new light by the rediscovery of the eschatological dimension of the Church at Vatican II, and especially stressed in the Constitution on the Church in the modern world, a Church 'going forward in the search for a future and abiding city.'

This primacy of the search for God characterizes the ideal of the monastic life which has not the secondary aim (teaching, nursing, preaching or other definite kind of apostolate) defining the modern Orders. On the other hand monastic life allows the search for God to take a great variety of form, some being more attracted by a life of silent prayer, others finding God more easily in liturgical praise and yet others in earnest working for the community and its spiritual and charitable services. These various vocations can be found in all the monasteries; their proportions vary and give to each house its particular character. This variety differentiates also monasticism from the contemplative orders which have been in evidence from the Middle Ages onwards and have generally chosen to stress the practice of one of these ways of contemplative prayer.

Texts[1]

Psalms: 41, 2–3; 44, 11; 62, 2; 104, 4.
Matt. 14, 23; Lk. 18, 28–30; Jn. 4, 23; Col. 3, 1–4; Acts. 2, 44–47; 21, 9
R.B. Prol. 3d Jan.; ch. 58, 11 Apr.
V. II. *Perfectae Caritatis* (P.C.). No. 7, 9.[*]
Lumen Gentium (L.G.). 38, 44

2. PEACE

Renouncing the world and dedicating one's life to the search for God is not enough: the main obstacles to the union with the divine are in the soul itself, often disturbed by many desires and passions. In the religions of the old Eastern cultures holy men already had this experience: the communion with the Absolute is the source of a perfect peace but it supposes a singleness of mind and a self-mastery which cannot be reached without a long and hard struggle. Restraint in food, celibacy, obedience to a Master, and the other ascetic practices aim at a discipline of mind and body which form the common background developed under various forms by Hindu Yogis and Sadhus, Jain, Buddhist and Muslim ascetics. They discovered methods for detaching one's mind from the external world, for disciplining the heart's desires and uniting the soul with the eternal.

Christian monks used the same general means but their researches were more directed toward a deep analysis of the human heart, its passions and tendencies, in order to discern between good and bad movements and the devil's temptations. A vigilant attention and a striving to master the passions develop virtues and lead step by step to peace of heart – the condition for union with God. Peace does not exclude combat, for our defects remain in ourselves, but peace grows as a fruit of this striving; it develops in love and in the unspeakable joy of union with God.

We must notice also that the biblical revelation and the light of Christ's Incarnation allowed Christians to get a well balanced appreciation of the real values present in the spiritual, corporal and worldly realities. Unlike many non-Christian ascetics, their striving does not imply any dualism or despising of the body and of the material world. The aim they search for is not liberation from matter but the perfect balance of mind and body often represented by the Fathers of the Church under the image of the 'natural state' of Adam and Eve in Paradise, before the Fall. There, all things were in harmony: human beings and nature, are linked to God, the centre and source of all good.

The daily struggle for self-mastery thus blossoms in peace

and purity of heart, it makes the soul attentive to the action of the Holy Spirit who attracts her into the interior self and opens the door for contemplation.

Texts

Mk. 1, 12–13; Lk. 9, 23; Jn. 12, 24.
Rom. 8, 13; Col. 3, 5; 2 Cor. 4, 10; 8, 2; 1 Pet. 4, 13.
R.B. Prol.; ch. 4; ch. 7.
V. II L.G. 46.

3. SILENCE

The concentration necessary to find in one's heart the contact with the Divine is helped by an external atmosphere of calm and silence. Ascetics belonging to all religions had this experience and we see them fleeing the cities to search God in the solitude of deserts and forests. A condition of union with God, silence is also one of the main components of the community life.

It is because the monks enable one another to live most easily and peacefully in solitude and silence, because they provide for one another an atmosphere of recollection and solitude and prayer, that they are able to achieve the supreme end of monastic life which is this spiritual and hidden banquet – the feast in which the Word sits down at table with His chosen ones and finds pleasure and consolation in their company. And He says: 'I have come into my garden ... I have eaten the honeycomb with my honey: I have drunk my wine with my milk: eat, O friends, and drink: be inebriated, O my dearly beloved'
(Canticle 5:1).
This is the true essential and perfect meaning of the common life. The monastery is a 'Tabernacle of the Testament' or, if you prefer, another upper room in which Jesus sits down at table with His disciples, nourishing them with His own substance which is the very Wisdom and Glory of God. The monastery is first and

above all a 'gate of heaven', a place where God comes down in His infinite charity to let Himself be seen and known by men. Everything vital and fruitful in the monastery derives its vitality from the fact that it contributes to this one essential end.

The silence of the forest, the peace of the early morning wind moving the branches of the trees, the solitude and isolation of the house of God: these are good because it is in silence, and not in commotion, in solitude and not in crowds, that God best likes to reveal Himself most intimately to men ...

In the common regular places of the monastery the silence and recollection with which the monks work, study and pray together enhances the whole atmosphere of silent work and prayer. The union of all these souls in a common effort, a common silence, and a single-minded charity makes the fruit of each one's prayers, merits and virtues become the spiritual possession of all

(Thomas Merton: *The Silent Life* p. 37–39).

What is true in the community life is true also on a broader scale for the Church at large. The search for God alone in solitude and silence, far from separating monks from their fellow men, 'unites them with their contemporaries in the heart of Christ' (L.G. 46). By its communion with others and its solitude monastic life witnesses that human life is both communion with God and with our fellow men, that the human heart should be open to others and always ready to receive in the depth of silence the Word of God who makes our lives fruitful and prepares the final encounter with the Divine Spouse.

Texts

I Kings 19, 11–12;
Hos. 2, 16; Is. 26, 20;
Lk. 5, 16; 6, 12;
Jam. 1, 25; 3, 2–10.

R.B. Silence requires an effort: ch. 7, 9°&11°; ch. 42 *studere* an atmosphere: ch. 22 'rising with all gravity and

restraint'; ch. 48, siesta and lectio; ch. 53 with guests; avoids sin: Prol. ch. 6 purifies thoughts and words: ch. 4 No. 50–54; ch. 49; nourished by the word of God: Prol. ch. 7, 1° introduction to intimate prayer: Prol. ch. 20; ch. 52; not to go out: ch. 4 (end); ch. 66.
V. II L. G. 46.
Eschatological sign: L.G. 8; 44; 48; *Gaudium et Spes* (G.S.) 1; 2; 3; 7; 8; 10; 12; 15; 22; 34; 38; 40; 45; 53; 56; 57; 59; 93.
Ad Gentes (A.G.) 2; 9.

4. HOSPITALITY

Silence understood as a meeting place for God and man implies the duty of welcoming men in the house of God. For St Benedict guests 'are never lacking in the monastery'. They are in some way members of the community, not for reason of stability but of passage. Stable monks and passing guests are like two complementary faces of Christ: Christ staying and welcoming, Christ knocking at the door and welcomed. It is this twofold presence which makes the monastery not the house of the monks but the house of God.

The welcome of guests has been made traditionally in several ways. People had already flocked to the Desert Fathers to receive spiritual guidance and encouragement; monasteries were also sometimes purposely placed along the pilgrims' roads to help them to cross difficult saddles in mountains or river fords. More generally they were placed at the outskirts of civilisation, in contact with it and nevertheless in solitude, in communion with men and orientated toward the search for God.

In our modern and materialistic times monasteries should be more then ever privileged places where the return to God is made easier. Their atmosphere of peace and prayer should help men coming for retreats or for a simple visit to appreciate not only the horizontal dimension of an equal charity for all, but the vertical dimension referring any human activity to God in a living and personal prayer, whether it be individual or common.

Besides receiving the poor who should have always the first place in our charity monks have thus a special duty to welcome the elites of all levels of their countries in order to help them to achieve the necessary distance from their daily life to be really themselves and conscious of what God asks from them. Another category of men toward whom monasteries have a special duty is the people of the neighbourhood: indeed the monastery is also a human place, part and parcel of a region, by which it must be adopted as a living and useful member.

Monasteries are also chosen places for the encounter of men of good will searching for God through different ways, for monks should strive to realise Ecumenism in their hearts as it was so well explained by Thomas Merton:

> If I can unite in myself the thought and devotion of Eastern and Western Christendom, the Greek and Latin Fathers, the Russian with the Spanish mystics, I can prepare in myself the reunion of divided Christians ... We must contain all divided worlds and transcend them in Christ. (Conjectures p. 12.)

It could be said also that it is not merely a question of uniting in oneself all the particular ways in order to assist the world and the Church to discover their unity, but to discover the source from which they spring, and there, in the Absolute of their very centre to achieve this work in unity.

Finally we must add that in many Asian countries, a large portion of the non-Christians draw their spiritual life from monastic spirituality, still a living tradition in their monasticism. Christian monasticism above all other forms of religious life puts before them a form of Christian life acceptable to them and capable of bringing their own spiritual aspirations to fulfilment in Christ. Hence their special duty to be open to this kind of dialogue.

Texts

Mt. 10, 8; Mk. 10, 44–45; Lk. 6, 27–31; Mt. 5, 42; Mk. 12, 30–33; 10, 42.

Ro. 12, 9–21; 15, 1–2; 2 Co. 13, 11; 1 Co. 13, 1–3;
Gal. 6, 3.
R. B. ch. 53. V. II. P. C. 9. A. G. 15.

5. WORK

A form of unworldliness practised mostly by non-Christian monks is begging, depending on others for all their necessities. But work also has been considered as a means of spiritual perfection, so much so that it became one of the traditional duties of Christian monks.

St Paul was always proud of the fact that what was necessary for the maintenance of himself and of his co-workers was met by the work of his own hands. He demanded of his Christians that they too follow his example, namely that they should work in order not to be a burden to others, but, on the contrary, to be able to help the needy. Monks from the very beginning took to heart this duty and St Benedict echoes the whole monastic tradition when he says: 'Then they are truly monks when they live by the labour of their hands like our Fathers and the Apostles'. But beside this essential notion, monastic work has a rich spiritual background.

Curiously enough it seems that work was taken up at first by the Desert Fathers as a help to prayer. During their long hours of solitary meditation a simple work like plaiting baskets or making ropes helped them to avoid distraction: it was like an 'anchor for thoughts'. Later on they divided their time between vocal prayer and work, this alternation making the concentration on God easier.

They discovered also that work develops some special virtues like humility, generosity, obedience, detachment and purity of heart. It is also a useful means for fighting against some temptations like sadness and despondency.

Zeal for working hard has also other motives. It is a penance, the most humble and simple way to master oneself and make atonement for our sins and others'. For the monk living in solitude, to share with his fellow men the hard burden of working in order to earn his daily living is one of

the best means of communion with them; it enables him to
offer all human suffering to God in remission for the sins of
the world.

But since the beginning, monks wanted to go beyond this
penitential level. They worked, then, so as to be able to give
in charity and help others. The first monasteries known in
history already supported alms houses and hospitals in the
cities, beside helping the poor of their neighbourhood. This
work can be manual as well as intellectual, depending on the
necessities of the place and of the abilities of the monks. But
it implies always respect and even love for the things used,
not for their own sakes but for the sake of God to whom they
belong. Everything used by a monk, from the simplest tools
and kitchenware to the highest concepts of art and philosophy should sing God's glory through the careful way and the
concern for beauty with which they are handled.

Work has also its own dangers: practised without
measure it can be a cause of dissipation and worldly cares
which are very harmful for the monastic vocation. That is
why monastic Rules insist on 'discretion'. They request the
Superiors to see that monks have a balanced activity so
necessary to keep the peace of heart and the presence of
God. For the same reason works have to be chosen which
are compatible with the life in a monastery:

> Everything in the monastery, then, is ordered to produce
> the atmosphere propitious for a life of prayer. The isola-
> tion of the monastery itself, the work by which the monks
> strive to be self-supporting and independent of secular
> contacts, the reading and study which are done in the clois-
> ter or in the cell, and the office chanted in choir all have for
> their function to keep the monastery what it is meant to be:
> a sanctuary where God is found and known, adored and, in
> a certain way, 'seen' in the darkness of contemplation
>   (Thomas Merton, *The Silent Life*, p. 33–34).

Texts

Ec. 7, 15; Ex. 20, 9; 1 Thes. 2, 9; 4, 11;
2 Thes. 3, 10–13; Act. 20, 34;

R. B. ch. 48, Mar.; ch. 57; ch. 66. discretion ch. 41. ch. 53;
ch. 64. respect: ch. 31.
V. II. P. C. 9.

6. VARIOUS FORMS OF MONASTIC LIFE

We have seen that suppleness and variety of forms was one
of the characteristics of monasticism. It appears not only in
the various aspects of the community life but also, at the
institutional level, in the different ways of practising
monastic life.

The 'cenobitic' or community life is the best known of the
monastic institutions. Its main advantage is the mutual help
in seeking God more earnestly. Mutual service and work in
the house:

> divides and distributes the burdens of material life,
> distributes the cares and responsibilities so that no one
> monk has too many material things to think about. Each
> one contributes his share in peace and recollection
> without undue anxiety
> (Thomas Merton, *The Silent Life* p. 38).

Community life is also
> a school of affection, fidelity and mercy. By sharing the
> prayers, labours and trials of our brothers and knowing
> them as they are, we learn to respect them and love them
> with a sober compassion that is too deep for sentimental-
> ity. We learn to be faithful to them. Depending on them,
> we know that they have a right to depend on us. We try
> to learn how not to fail them. Finally we forgive others
> their faults and sins against us, as we ourselves would be
> forgiven by them and by God. In this school of charity
> and peace a man learns not only to respect and to love
> others, but also, in the purest sense, to love and respect
> his own person for the sake of God
> (Thomas Merton, *The Silent Life*, p. 45).

This earnest desire of God, of being united with him by love gives sense to what monks call 'the good of obedience'. As I love Him above all, I want to do at any cost what He wants of me. The problem is to know His will. The whole organisation of the monastery is meant to make this knowledge easy for all. First there are the general rules which are nothing but the concrete application of the Gospel to daily life. Then the role of the Superior is to make unity in the community by helping each one and the whole group to discover and follow God's will. He is assisted in this task by various councils of brothers and is asked to study carefully each case, by talks and personal contacts with the individuals concerned. The decision taken before God, after all possible human care, can safely be believed to be for God's will for the monk, and followed freely with all his heart.

> This theology of the common life is, paradoxically, the justification for the presence of solitaries in the monastic body. The solitary vocation is rare today, but that does not mean that it does not exist at all, still less that it has no longer any reason for existing ... It is quite logical that one member or another of a Benedictine or Cistercian community be allowed by his Abbot, after a careful testing of his vocation, to separate himself in some measure from the rest to devote himself more fully to prayer. He may be less visibly engaged in the exterior manifestation of the common life, but he fulfils his function well and becomes a more fruitful agent in the common life, he enters, as it were, into the spiritual heart of the common life by attaining more perfectly to the common end for which the whole community is striving
> (Thomas Merton, *The Silent Life*, p. 40–41).

Actually it seems that the first monks were hermits, some of them in huts, others wandering in the deserts or begging in the villages. Many also lived a semi-eremitic life, meeting only on Sundays for Mass and making provision for food and for material for work. Others finally lived in small groups of two or three together.

In our days the renewal of contemplation brought also a renewal of eremitic life and the desire of small communities in order to stress the search for God as Absolute and the primacy of contemplation. It is indeed easier for individuals or small groups to witness to the simplicity, poverty and renunciation of the Gospel which is the great concern of the Church today.

A consequence of the plurality of forms taken by monastic life is its faculty of adaptation. History shows that monks, though very faithful to their stability in their monastery undertook innumerable kinds of work and apostolate according to the necessities of their time and places.

This suppleness allowed also Christian monastic life to be at ease in all the cultures known up to our days: Jewish, Hellenic, Syriac, African, Roman, European, American, etc. It faces now anew both the old Eastern civilisations, which have been the cradle of the monastic institution, and the new peoples of other continents in which it was quite unknown. It belongs to the monks of our days to realise this anew in the light of the old experiences.

Texts

Community life: Jn. 6, 37; 15, 17; 1 Co. 1, 10–11; Tit. 3, 2;
Obedience: Jn. 4, 34; 14, 21; 14, 31; 15, 10; Mt. 12, 50; Lk.
1, 38; Heb. 5, 8–9; Phil. 8, 9;
R. B. ch. 1; ch. 5; ch. 68; ch. 71; ch. 72.
V. II. P.C. 2 (Introd.) 9 (end); 7.
A.G. 10; 11; 18; 26; 40.
P.C. 1; 2.

7. KOINONIA

Cenobites have often been defined as those who live in common, under a Rule and an Abbot. Rules and spiritual Masters are found in all forms of monastic life Christian and non-Christian. The search for the Absolute is a difficult and sometimes dangerous path in which it is imprudent to go along without a guide and without a certain knowledge of the spiritual and psychological laws governing the human mind.

Common life, as a means leading to union with God,

seems to be an idea especially developed in Christianity. It was called *Koinonia* by the very first monastic community (that of Pachomius in Egypt) and the name has been retained with that particular meaning.

Pachomius did not imagine that he was creating a new concept when he proposed to his monks the ideal of the *Holy Koinonia*, the peaceful and supernatural mutual love. It was the special commandment of Jesus, repeated by the Apostles and lived by the first Christians at Jerusalem. The Desert Fathers themselves stressed the importance of that virtue: the main lesson St Antony learned from his first visit to the Egyptian solitary monk was 'devotion to Christ and mutual love'. In the desert the neighbour was seldom physically met but he was often present in mind. To keep charity in one's heart, to avoid judging others, to be always ready to help and to give to the unexpected guest everything you have, supposes the Evangelical disposition of soul, well-spring of all the acts of charity. So it is not surprising to see, in the writings of those hermits that charity is among the topics the most frequently treated. They wanted to practise to the full, according to their vocation, the twofold command of love of God and love of the neighbour.

The genius of Pachomius is to have applied that doctrine of community life. As charity is the fulness of the law, and the edification of others an essential precept, to be a cause of sadness for another Brother is a fault. On the contrary all have to become by love one another's servants; peace with the Brethren is the warrant of the peace with God. The harmony of the heavenly society is the model of community life.

St Basil on his side stressed the advantages of common life for spiritual improvement: fraternal love helps in seeking one's faults and in eradicating them; it gives opportunities for practising virtues, especially that of charity and, through it, for proving one's love for God.

The monastic tradition up to our times has unfolded the various aspects of this theme. It revealed the monastery as the meeting point of two currents, both carrying monks to God through complementary means.

The first one, often called 'vertical' is the direct ascent of the soul to God. The common goal, which in the monastery welds the individuals together, is not external activities but the search for the love of God, pure charity. In that perspective the Abbot is seen as Christ's representative and the minister of God's will; the Rule is meant to create the proper environment for the normal growth of each vocation.

But monastic life is not simply a secret dialogue between the soul and God, it is a turning together towards God and a sharing of this experience; hence the horizontal current of approach to God through the members of the spiritual family of the Brethren headed by the 'Father Abbot'. The individual transformation is made through the incorporation into a given community. The vows of 'conversion of life' and 'stability' stress this permanent effort of union with and imitation of Christ present among men, obedient to his Father and to local authority, humble of heart and meek towards all. The transcendent God is thus found in a tangible way in the neighbour through acts of mutual obedience and charity.

The presence of Christ in the individual members of the community affects also the role of the monastic Superior. One of his main functions is to create harmony and consensus in the community. It will not be done by authoritative decisions but by consulting, in an exchange of values and response. St Benedict specifies: 'The reason why we said that all should be called for counsel is that the Lord often reveals to the younger what is the best.' In the same way when somebody has to be corrected the Abbot should trust in God's grace always at work in men's hearts and 'at the example of the Good Shepherd, ... carry back the delinquent to the flock' by 'comforting him ... and inducing him to make humble satisfaction'.

Christ's presence in others brings an atmosphere of peace and love which is both expressed and fostered by the kindness in mutual relations often described in St Benedict's Rule:

The juniors shall honour their seniors and the seniors

love their juniors ... Monks should bear with the greatest patience one another's infirmities whether of body or character and vie in paying obedience one to another. Let no one follow what seems good for himself but rather what is good for another. Let them practise fraternal charity with a pure love ... Let them prefer nothing whatever to Christ.

Sharing thus all the day long in Christ's life and having to give it to each other, monks are mutually responsible for their spiritual improvement. But their life is not closed, on themselves, it is a sharing in God's charity and it takes its infinite dimensions. Nowhere perhaps does the monastic community find a better expression than in the common prayer. United with the heavenly choirs, monks praise God in the name of the Universe; participating in Christ's life-giving Sacrifice they are welded in a common love and with Him they embrace the whole world and offer it to God.

Texts

The first commandment: Mk. 12, 30–33; Jn. 13, 34–35; 15, 12–17; 17, 21–23; 1 Jn. 3, 4.
Forgiveness: Lk. 6, 26–31; Mt. 5, 20–26; 6, 11–15; 18, 21–22; 25, 40–45.

Notes

1   R.B. refers to the Rule of St Benedict. V. II. refers to the Documents of Vatican II.

CHAPTER 8

Convergences

In the themes of monastic spirituality we have already noticed many similarities between the monachisms of the different religions. It is worth delving into the matter, to find out what they all have in common. This research will, at the same time, point out some of the specifics of each religion, especially as regards Christianity.

The first, and probably the most fundamental and common aspect is that all monks are moving towards the same goal – the seeking of the Absolute. This search is the centre around which the different forms of monastic life can grow freely while remaining in harmony with each other.

This unique goal implies the use of similar means to reach it. All those who crave for the Absolute have experienced that the way they trod was hard, and sometimes dangerous. They have thus acknowledged the need for an experienced person who could guide and support them, and show the obstacles to be avoided.

Moreover, in all religions, the first stage of the spiritual journey is an effort to overcome vices, especially pride and lust, which tend towards worldly and transitory goods, and prevent the heart from looking at the Infinite.

This self-mastery is attained through an ascesis which controls all details of life by means of precise rules. The fact that such regulations are found in the monachisms of all religions shows that they are the fruit of experience, and so necessary for spiritual training.

Nevertheless, the external behaviour of the monk should be nothing but the expression of his interior quest; so the aim of ascesis is purification of heart. Indeed, the monk wants to smother in himself what the Buddhists call the 'desires', which, in many respects, corresponds to the 'old man' that St Paul wants Christians to put to death in themselves. Thus, the physical ascesis is complemented by an effort to hold the thoughts in check and, in a more positive way, by meditation, which strengthens the convictions, keeps a person away from evil and helps him to cling to his ideal. The methods leading to this goal differ widely as do their rational justifications. But these very divergences make still clearer the fundamental common point which Jesus expressed in saying: 'Blessed are the clean of heart, for they shall see God' (Mt 5, 8).

It should be noted here that celibacy is generally taken for granted in a life dedicated to the search of the Absolute. Celibacy is total and perpetual for those who think that their life ends in a meeting with the Absolute; such was the belief of the Jewish ascetics, and is still now that of the Hindus and Christians. Buddhists keep celibacy, as a rule, during their stay in monastic life. These facts seem to indicate that celibacy is essential for religious life, and that its questioning may be due to a slackening of the search for God.

Other signs of a genuine quest are also stressed by all religions, namely, perseverance and sincerity. It is obvious that a firm decision and strong will are needed to bear the strain of interior purification. In the same way, progress in monastic life supposes a single-minded effort and the absence of disguised selfishness. Pharisaism was criticised by Jesus, and the Fathers of the Church mercilessly denounced this defect when it appeared among their disciples. But, centuries before, the *Bhagavad-Gîta* and the Buddhist writings insisted on detachment. For them, it is also expressed by a request for sincerity in words and deeds which is one of the main aspects of non-violence, a typical monastic virtue of the East. This internal attitude should be reflected in the monk's behaviour, making him always benevolent and serene.

The study of the aspects common to all monasticism led us to point out some of the qualities proper to each of them. A closer look at Christian monasticism will allow us to discern its particular role in the Church, and to see how it differs from other religions.

The primacy of this search for God puts all other activities at a secondary level, thus distinguishing monasticism from other forms of Christian religious life, which are essentially dedicated to a specific apostolate. The monks' prayer gives fraternal support to others' striving for union with God, and asks him to make their apostolate fruitful.

The Christian monk still differs from ascetics of other religions by the position occupied by Christ in his search for the Absolute. Jesus, indeed, revealed that he is 'the way' leading to God; the only work of human spiritual guides is to lead men to listen to him 'the only true teacher'[1]. All human activities which take on his likeness are considered as good.

Furthermore, the Christian can meet God in Jesus, true man and true God. In his Lord, he contemplates body and spirit reconciled, and the created world becomes a means of union with the Infinite instead of being an obstacle to it. Thus, Christian ascesis will not seek to get away from matter, it will rather strive to make the body a docile instrument for the service of the Spirit and to recognise, in all worldly goods, the Infinite God who keeps them in existence.

Jesus also revealed the mystery of the Holy Trinity, which allows us to penetrate, as it were, into the intimate life of the Infinite. Through his teaching, we learn that the Ocean of Peace is not a kind of neutral infinitude to be reached through supreme stripping of the self, but rather, an immense current of love in which we are carried towards the Father, through the Spirit, in an endless exchange of joy. Christian monastic life will thus be a search for union with Christ, which starts here below in mutual love and progressively transforms the monk into his image, and makes him share the divine life. The Christian can thus use all the means of purification and concentration discovered by the different religions, provided he uses them to remove the obstacles which prevent him from opening himself to the action of Christ's Spirit.

Jesus also taught us that 'all that you do to the least of

mine, you do it to me'. This truth gives a new dimension to human relationships and particularly, to community life in monasticism. Buddha had already stressed the necessity of good relations between the members of his communities. But it seems that he aimed to give each one the peace needed for his interior quest. Christians meet God in the people they serve for the love of Christ. That is why, in the monastic tradition, fraternal charity is placed beside asceticism as a means of union with God. This care for others finds its expression in the prayer of the Church for the whole world. The most isolated hermit feels himself to be connected with and responsible for all human beings before God. Withdrawal from the world is not an escape from its problems but a necessity, allowing the monk to keep a certain distance, so that he can more easily receive, in the silence of his heart, the concerns of mankind, and bring them to God. Monasteries have always been centres of hospitality and Antony, the great solitary, was called 'spiritual physician of Egypt'.

The Fathers of the Church understood the role of monastic life as an imitation of Christ praying on the mountain, and of the angels who stand constantly before the throne of God in an attitude of love and worship. The monks share in their work of guarding the Church and are like 'ramparts protecting the cities'.[2]

Here is the final convergence and common role of monastic life in all religions. Centred on the search for the Absolute, it stands as a sign, reminding mankind that the aim of human life is not possession of perishable goods but rather, to become one day, 'citizens of heaven',[3] a privilege that all can begin to enjoy, here and now, through an intimate contact with the Divine Presence, which dwells in the depth of the heart.

Notes

1   Origen, *In 2 Co.* and *Scholia in Apocalyps. IX.*
2   St John Chrysostom, *In Matt.*, Hom. 72, 4.
3   St John Chrysostom, *In Matt. Hom.* 8, 4.

Present state of the Monastic Orders in the Catholic Church

BENEDICTINE monasteries are generally grouped in congregations federated under an Abbot Primate. We have no statistics for the others. There are two orders of CISTERCIANS, one of them is organised in Congregations, the other is that of the 'Strict Observance', commonly called 'Trappists'.

EASTERN MONASTERIES are under the authority of the local bishops. We have asked information from the fifteen patriarchates and received answers from the Ecumenical Patriarchate of Istanbul and from those of Jerusalem, Romania and of the territories of the Czechs and Slovaks. We give the total numbers of these four patriarchates.

BENEDICTINE MONKS

Confederated:	23 Congregations	223 monasteries	8,694 monks

CISTERCIAN MONKS

Trappist		96	2,552
Others	10	91	1,279

EASTERN MONKS

4 Patriarchates	215	3,500
Mt Athos		1,500

BENEDICTINE Women

Nuns	354	7,642
Sisters	485	10,250

CISTERCIAN Women

Trappistines	66	1,883
Others	64	1,085

EASTERN NUNS

	c250	4,960

Appendix II: Chronology

Dates BC	Bible	Other Religions	Historical Events
2500		1st Egypt, monotheistic devotional texts, Ptah-hotep. King Meri-cara c. 2100 BC	Harappa culture Eg 3rd Dynasty
1900	Abraham	Rig Veda	Code of Hammurabi
			Aryan invasions in India
		Eg. Scribe Anii	Trojan war
			Philistines in Palestine
			Tel el Amarana let.
1300	Moses	Eg. Amenope	
1000	David		
800	Prophets Elijah		
700	Isaiah		
600	Exile to Babylon	Earliest Upanishads Mahavira (Jainism) 599–527	Cyrus unites the Medes and the Persians

500BC		Gautama Buddha 540–480 Pythagoras Lao Tsu Confucius d. 479	Xerxes wars with Greece
400		Plato	
300		Zeno (Stoic school) Bhagavad Gita Introduction of Buddhism in Ceylon	Alexander the Great Asoka c. 269
200	Septuagint at Alexandria	Eg devotees in Serapis temple Beginning of Mahayana Buddhism	
100	Book of Wisdom made in Egypt	Essenes (Qumran) Therapeutes at Alexandria Buddhism in China AD 25	Augustus Emperor Philo
Christ AD	New Testament Virgins and *Continentes*	Bud. Pali Scriptures AD 80	Capture of Jerusalem by Titus AD 70
100		Nagarjuna (Bud.) d 150	

Dates	E. Churches	W. Churches	Other Rel.	Hist. Events
200AD	Clement d. 215 Origen d. 253 Antony 251–356 Syriac Hermits	Tertullian d. 220 Cyprian d. 258 Hermits & Virgins in Italy, Gaul, Spain		Persecutions
300AD	Pachomius'Rule c.315 Amoun at Nitria 330 Macarius at Scete c.330 Estathius of Sebaste c.355 Ephrem d. 373 Basil d. 379 Found.mon. Mt. Sinai, 380 Jerome at Bethlehem, 386 Gregory Naz. d. 390 Gregory Nys. d. 394	Hilary d. 371 Eusebius of V.d.371 Ambrose d.397 Martin d. 397	Gupta Age in India 320–467	Constantine Emp.312, end of persecutions

				Great Invasions in Europe
400AD	Euthymius d. 405 John Chrysostom d. 407 Simeon Stylites d. 412 Theodoret's hist 440 Found Stoudios mon 463 Diadochus of P d. 480	Found.Lérins mon. 410 Jerome d. 420 Augustine d. 430 Paulinus of N d. 431 Cassian d. 435 Patrick d. 461 Faustus of R d. 490	Vasulbandhu (Bud) c. 400 1st Catalogue of Bud. Tripitaka (518)	Rome taken by Alaric 410 Council of Chalcedon 450
500	Pseudo-Dionysius St Sabas d. 532 Dorotheus of G c 550 Cyril of S. d. 560	Caesarius of A d. 543 St Benedict d. 547 St Gregory's *Dial* St Augustine of C in England 596	Bodhidharma in China 520 Bud. in Japan 552	Clovis bapt. c. 500 Gothic war in Italy 535–555 Emp Justinian d. 565
600	John Moschus d. 620 John Climacus d. 649 Maximus the C. d. 662	St Columbanus d. 615 St Isidore of S. d. 636 Synod of Whitby 663 St Hilda d. 680	Alvars 6th to 10th cent. Tamil Shaiva Sts 7th-8th cent Beginning of	Mohammed leaves Mecca for Medina the era of Hegira begins 622

Dates	E. Churches	W. Churches	Other Rel.	Hist. Events
700	St J. Damascene d. 754	St Bede the V d. 735 St Willibrord d. 739 St Boniface d. 754	Tib. Bud. Sch. Nyingmapa 1st Sufi organisation Sankara 788–820	Capture of Alexandr. by Muslims 642 Conquest of North Africa 698 Muslims rch.Ind. 712
800 AD	St Theodore Studite d. 826	Alcuin d. 804 St Benedict of A. d. 821 St Ansgar d. 865	Rabi'a d. 801 (Suf) Tibet Sch. Sakyapa and Kagyupa	Battle of Poitiers 732 stops their progress in Western Europe 800 Charlem. Emp. Norman raids
900	1st mon. Mt Athos 963	Found. Cluny 910 St Dunstan d. 987	Al Junaid d. 910 (Suf) Al Hallaj d. 922 Ibn Al Arabi d. 956	Otto I Emp. of W.
1000	St Simeon the New Theol d. 1022 In Russia: St Antony of Kiev d. 1073	St Romuald d. 1027 St Peter Dam. d. 1072 John of Fécamp d. 1078		1054 Schism E-W

	St Theodose d. 1074	Found. of Carthusians by St Bruno 1084 Found. of Cîteaux 1098		1st Crusade 1095
1100		St Anselm d. 1109 St Bernard d. 1153 St Peter the V. d. 1156 St Elizabeth of Shon. d. 1164 St Hilegarde d. 1179	Al Gazali d. 1111 Ramanjua d. 1137 Nimbarka	Jerus. is taken again by Muslims (Saladin) 1187
1200		St Dominic d. 1221 St Francis of A d. 1226 St Ludgarde d. 1246 St Sylvester d. 1267	Zen Sch. Soto Dogen d. 1253 Sch. Rinzai Jalai al Din-Rumi d. 1273 Madhva d. 1278	Mongol invasions in East Europe
1300	Gregory Palamas d. 1359	St Mechtilde d. 1290 St Gertrude d. 1302 St Bernard Ptolomei d. 1349	Ramananda Kabir Tibet Sch. Gelugpa	Black Death in Eur.

Dates	E. Churches	W. Churches	Other Rel.	Hist. Events
1400	Monastic development in Russia	1st Benedictine Congregations Julian of N.d. 1414 S Francesca Romana d. 1440		Constantinople capt. by Turks 1453
1500AD		1st mon. in Brazil	Vallabha d. 1531 Caitanya d. 1537 Guru Nanak (Sikh) d. 1538	Luther d. 1546 Dissolution of mon. in Britain (Henry VIII) d. 1549 Council of Trent 1545–1663
1600	1st Maronite Cong. 1695 1st Melkite Cong. 1697	New Congreg. in Europe (St Maur etc) La Trappe English mon. on the Continent	Tulsidas d. 1623 Tukaram d. 1649 5th Dalai Lama King of Tibet 1642	
1700	Armenia Mekitarist Congregation 1717 Philocalia 1782			French Rev. 1789

1800	Dev. of monasticism in Russia New Cong. in Lebanon and for Chaldaeans Charbel Maklouf d. 1898	Mon. revival Western Europe Foundations in North America	Ramakrishna d. 1896	
1900	New start in Western Europe and North America	New Benedictine Cong. and development of Trappists in North America Numerous foundations in Mission territories	Vivekananda d. 1902 Rabindranath Tagore d. 1941 Mahatma Gandhi d. 1948 Sri Aurobindo d. 1950	Russian Rev. 1917 Invasion of Tibet by China 1949